T0197441

LISTENING TO
MILLENNIALS:
56 PRICELESS TIPS FOR
MANAGERS

LISTENING TO
MILLENNIALS:
56 PRICELESS TIPS FOR
MANAGERS

MALATI SHINAZY;
AMANDA DIEFENDERFER

BALBOA
PRESS

A DIVISION OF HAY HOUSE

Balboa Press books may be ordered through booksellers or by contacting:

Balboa Press
A Division of Hay House
1663 Liberty Drive
Bloomington, IN 47403
www.balboapress.com
1 (877) 407-4847

Because of the dynamic nature of the Internet, any web addresses or links contained in this book may have changed since publication and may no longer be valid. The views expressed in this work are solely those of the authors and do not necessarily reflect the views of the publisher, and the publisher hereby disclaims any responsibility for them.

The intent of the authors is only to offer information of a general nature to help you in your professional development. In the event you use any of the information in this book for yourself, which is your constitutional right, the authors and the publisher assume no responsibility for your actions.

Print information available on the last page.

ISBN: 978-1-5043-5520-9 (sc)
ISBN: 978-1-5043-5525-4 (hc)
ISBN: 978-1-5043-5524-7 (e)

Library of Congress Control Number: 2016906020

Balboa Press rev. date: 06/01/2016

Dedicated to stalwart managers everywhere.

Foreword

Over the past quarter century I have personally hosted interns in my workplace, who now represent close to a score of different nations, readying themselves to seek an entry-level or new job, or hoping to get some international experience that would help them on their way. For almost this entire period, Malati Shinazy has been at times a near-at-hand colleague, and at other times a virtual collaborator in our common mission of creating resources for cultural competence.

We have watched these younger people, sometimes enjoying them, sometimes puzzled by them, but always learning from their cultural and personal characteristics. It is only over the years that we began to see certain patterns of difference emerge that we now know that we need to explore using the framework of generational cultural dynamics if we are to learn how we might best manage, mentor, and motivate them and help them succeed. Our own competence and success as managers unconditionally demands this.

This book provides managers with simple and direct insights and advice about collaborating with millennials, who now make up the largest contingent of the workforce. While a generational culture does in fact create and promote the values and rules that lead to survival and success for its members in their specific environment, these are only abstractions.

They are distilled from a rich puree of conversations and stories that members of this culture embrace as their own, as well as spill out about themselves in words and comportment, stories about who they are on the way to becoming and who they need to be.

Fortunately, *Listening To Millennials* is replete with first-hand stories and quotations from millennials themselves, as well as from others' experiences of them, making it both easily understandable and, more importantly, actionable. A good part of this immediacy is due to the close collaboration of the second author, Amanda Diefenderfer, who serves as a cultural informant both in research leading up to the writing of this book, and in her reflective consciousness of her own first-hand, personal experience as a millennial.

I am delighted to see this book appear, convinced that it and the many tips it provides will be invaluable for not only managers of other ages like myself, but also because it provides a framework and workspace for understanding, reflection, and discussion, which can also be used for training room exercises and academic education, assisting all generations to better know and appreciate each other.

– Dr. George F. Simons,
Founder and editor-in-chief of diversophy®, and lecturer in international management

Acknowledgements

No one achieves anything worth accomplishing alone. Many people helped move this book from concept to print.

Nikie Chapman Bauer inspired the initial idea. Malati's daughter, Greer, functioned as a muse, advisor, and editor. Linda S. Clark designed our chapter illustrations. Author photos were taken by Pam Forrest and John Patrick Images. Bob Millavec, Peter Houck, and Ron Vieira provided copyediting assistance. Amanda's parents and Malati's grandparents instilled in us deeply held values which pushed us to complete the project, albeit slowly, and despite the multitude of challenges of daily business requirements, family obligations, and inevitable detours. Jean Guillaume and Joe provided each of us time, space, meals, and encouragement.

Thanks to each of you for your unique contributions.

– Malati and Amanda

Contents

Chapter One

CONFESSIONS OF A BABY BOOMER MANAGER: A BOOK IS BORN

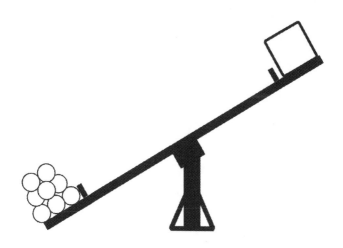

"This woman is driving me crazy. If she hates her job so much, why doesn't she just quit?" Did that thought come from me? Well, yes, actually it did. I am a goal-driven, get-it-done manager. And, I wanted to scream almost daily each time I heard from my twenty-four-year-old administrative assistant:

> *"I just got my bachelor's degree. I should be running a department, not just being an administrative assistant!"*

Eventually, I would cool off and no longer consider the silly idea of jumping out of our office windows. Yes, that is how desperate I felt. We were on the first floor and the windows did not open! Still, for a nanosecond, I would imagine myself diving right through them, screaming, just to get away from her incessant complaining.

When she stopped and I calmed down, I would sit down and chat with her and acknowledge her perception and needs, putting to use all the active listening skills I had been practicing for decades. I tried to assuage her restlessness by telling her that we all started somewhere, we all "paid our dues" and moved into jobs requiring increasing responsibility. I encouraged her to shadow other staff in our department and elsewhere in the company. I suggested she take free online classes in the field of her choice in order to boost her qualifications for higher-level jobs. I told her everything I heard when I was a young employee and promised to do anything she needed to help her progress. But still she groused and grumbled. Meanwhile, I inwardly cycled through the four versions of expressionist painter Edvard Munch's painting, *The Scream.*

In due course, she quit and I hired an assistant ten years her senior. Whew, I realized after a few weeks – everything was getting done and the entire team was now a group of relatively happy campers. There are always going to be process and deadline stressors at work, and our department was no different than any other in this regard. However, these stressors now existed without the daily verbal laments and contagious unhappiness of one young employee.

A few years later in the learning and talent development department at another company I had the opportunity to do the millennial employee and baby boomer manager dance again. This time, however, my millennial staff member, Nikie, wanted more. She was indeed the sponge my executive vice president of human resources told me she was. I was in awe of her, and yet again I was inwardly screaming. My sense of self as the perfect manager was shattered. I knew something was going on that I had better figure out before this hyper-productive and sensitive wizard brought my entire department down. Or worse, she would quit, taking her brilliant talent with her.

On the way to work one day, dreading whatever fussing I was going to have to face from anyone at the office that day, I had a moment of clarity. The voice of my mentor, Dr. George F. Simons, whispered to my manager brain:

> *"This is a cultural diversity clash! You are a diversity and inclusion expert. Treat the situation the way you would any other diversity challenge."*

I remembered his definition of culture:

> *"Culture is a set of rules, developed by a group of people for survival and success."*

My epiphany? My young employee and I were in the same work group, with the same business goals, and spoke the same American English. However, we were operating from different cultures!

As the manager, I needed figure out the rules for survival and success for this bright go-getter or she would be off to another job at a competing company. The truism, "employees quit managers, not companies," replaced my inner scream. With determination, I decided not to let that happen. As in the classic cultural iceberg, a person's behavior represents only 10 percent of who they are. The other 90 percent is under the water line, invisible. I needed to understand what was below the actions and behavior I was witnessing from Nikie. From understanding her multi-dimensional cultural beliefs, values, biases, attitudes, and perceptions – as well as developing a better understanding of my own – I could start building a cultural bridge on which we could both work well together.

...

Priceless Tip #1

Use the cultural iceberg framework to understand your millennial employee on a deeper level. It is more effective than inwardly screaming.

...

I read all the academic, big consulting company, and government studies on employees alternately known as the "millennial generation," "generation y," or the "echo generation."

I chatted with other managers about what they were doing to work effectively with the members of this group of young employees. More often than not, I heard frustrated variations of what the academic data was telling us, that these employees are a challenge to manage. Here is one such comment:

"I don't call them the 'millennial generation.' I call them the 'entitlement generation.' They want everything! And they want it now!"

...

Priceless Tip #2

Do not hesitate to ask peers for their ideas. Just don't be surprised if they know less than you do.

...

With a lot of effort and sincere dialogue, my young employee and I developed a highly productive working relationship. She told me that she did not want to be just a sponge. She wanted to be squeezed, challenged, and given more responsibility with mission-critical assignments.

I started to look for such opportunities for her. I set clear outcome expectations, coached her a little, provided her with resources, and then let her run — yet was always available to answer her questions in a text message or within our weekly one-on-one meetings. Sometimes, I just needed to provide her with reassurance that she was on the right track.

...

Priceless Tip #3

Sincere dialogue means we listen deeply more than we speak.

...

Within months Nikie was ready to lead a cross-functional project team with employees who outranked me in the company organization chart. I attended the first meeting and informed the project team that Nikie was taking the lead and I would be supporting the project in the background but not attending future meetings. The look on the faces of the vice president and senior vice president is embedded in my mind's eye. I can only imagine they were thinking, "You are the manager. She is just a specialist. And we are suppose to follow her?" I am sure those thoughts were followed by a bit of inner huffing and puffing.

Of course, I kept my finger on the pulse of the project, continually checking in and occasionally attending a meeting to be sure we were meeting our milestones. The result? The project was handed off to the next team in the project process on time and with superior quality. Nikie and I were both proud of her achievements.

We did more than successfully bridge the culture gap as manager and millennial employee. Over time, we became mentor and protégée, and eventually, friends. She is a wise young woman, and I learned as much from Nikie as she did from me. Additionally, our team culture took on a whole new feel as we succeeded in strengthening our relationships. There was a sense of healthy curiosity about the values and cultural needs of each colleague.

Our success as a collaborative team culture became increasingly more evident in our daily performance and in the agility of our informal interactions. As the work of any learning and talent development department requires a fair share of online research for instructional content, someone on the team would inevitably stumble upon one of the thousands of personality surveys on the web such as, "What Kind Of Insect Are You?" Sharing these with each other became a light-hearted way to break up the day. And, when one of us learned an important skill or concept, it too became known to us all.

...

Priceless Tip #4

Remember this useful definition of culture: "A set of rules developed by a group of people for survival and success." From this definition you will not only gain greater understanding of yourself and your millennial employees, you can also lead the development of your team's optimal working culture.

...

Malati's Background

I come from a multiethnic, multiracial, multicultural family. I was curious about other cultures before I even knew what the word meant. Cultural anthropology was one of my minors as an undergraduate student. I have always been curious about people's stories and have a thirst to know the "why" behind big data. As a young woman I wanted to investigate people in the field, like cultural anthropologist Margaret Meade (1901-1978) who studied the people of the South Pacific and Southeast Asia.

Without needing to travel quite so far, I found opportunities for cultural exploration within my own community. In an earlier stage of my career, I worked with high school students to develop the learning game TeenDIVERSOPHY™, which focuses on teaching thirteen- to nineteen-year-olds the skills they need to thrive in their diverse communities. Without realizing it, this work provided my first "Margaret Meade" moments. The content for TeenDIVERSOPHY™ was written for teens by teens, and gave me the opportunity to learn what was important to them, in the field of their own high school environments.

Over the course of several academic years, different groups of high school students wrote, field tested, and edited the content of the game. One group struggled over how to word the content of the game's cards so their peers across the nation could learn the skills of living in our increasingly diverse world. They were disappointed when they discovered that at ages fourteen and fifteen, most high school freshmen were too young to understand some of the critical thinking questions in the game. And, they were thrilled to learn that a local university planned to use the game as part of college freshman orientation week. They were excited and a bit scared, as was I, because the game had not yet been field tested with college-aged teens. As they watched the seventeen- to nineteen-year-old college students play the game, they took notes for improving it.

Together, we learned how to make the content clearer and simpler so it would be useful for a more diverse audience, for teens that came from many different demographic groups and regions of the US. TeenDIVERSOPHY™ will always be a work in progress, as each generation of teens is unlike the previous one. Their concerns about topics of diversity and inclusion will naturally evolve as their world does.

Another "aha!" moment for me was when I realized that the TeenDIVERSOPHY™ developers are the millennials we are writing about now! The teenagers that wrote the original content for TeenDIVERSOPHY™ have been in the workplace for just over a decade. So emerged another opportunity to learn about this same age cohort – in a new stage of their lives.

Overcoming my own struggle to become a great manager for millennials was just one step towards sharing my knowledge and insights with other managers. The original idea for this book was inspired by my relationship with my former employee Nikie, who became my coauthor of choice. As a businesswoman, I knew that partnering with this smart, insightful, and results-oriented young woman as a coauthor would simply make for a better book.

I then met Amanda, who helped me with projects for my consulting business. I was stunned and shocked. Here is another one! She is from the millennial generation, she is brilliant, her command of written language is amazing, and she is ambitious. Coauthor Number Two? You bet.

Our ultimate goal with this book is to help managers become the best managers they can with their millennial employees. We want to help managers create workplace environments in which millennial employees can thrive, be happy, and do their best work. Their work satisfaction and high engagement is bound to be contagious to other employees. The return on investment (ROI) will include reduced turnover, greater productivity, and higher engagement and innovation. The term "engagement" has become almost a cliché in business; so we have given it an operational definition:

> *"An employee is engaged when s/he demonstrates consistent enthusiasm and commitment to meet individual, group, and organizational goals, embraces learning and personal/professional growth, and co-creates a pleasant work environment for the work group."*

...

Chapter One Bonus Exercise

Frame the frustrations you may be feeling managing your millennial employees as growing pains. Often, if we do not recognize that something is not working, we will not search for solutions to improve it. That you are reading this book indicates you are on the continuous process-improvement journey – the process of becoming a more effective manager. Congratulate yourself!

... ...

Chapter Two

WE CAN'T WRITE THE BOOK YET: THE RESEARCH PHASE

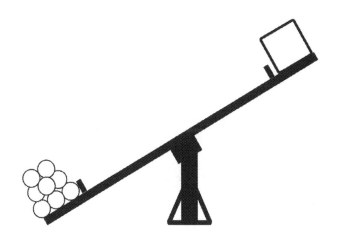

As the largest employee group in the US workforce, it is not surprising that big data has extensively researched millennials. Organizations such as the US Census Bureau, US Chamber of Commerce, Pew Research Center, the Society for Human Resources Management, and the Council of Economic Advisors for the President of the United States have published studies on millennial numbers, opinion, and impact on economics.

Academic research is hefty too. Anick Tolbize's work for the Research and Training Center on Community Living at the University of Minnesota provided a comprehensive review of the literature in *Generational Differences In The Workplace*.

Below is a quick summary of her work and the research of her peers on the early influencers of this group of nearly eighty million US millennial employees.

...

The Common Growing-Up Experience

- Over one-third had divorced parents or parents who never married

- Over two-thirds had both parents in the workplace

- They were the first full generation of latchkey children
  - They learned at a young age how to be self-sufficient
  - Non-school time was highly scheduled

- Many had parents who exercised the parenting style of "quality over quantity"
  - Some parents were highly indulgent

- Collaborative learning was the rule at school
  - Students worked together rather than independently

- Boosting self-esteem took the form of:
  - Everyone is a winner
  - Everyone gets an award

- Television and DVDs were babysitters
  - They watched between 2-4 hours of programming each day

- ○ 30 minute TV programs were interrupted by up to 15 advertising commercials

- They were babies or young children when home computers and video games became mainstream

...

Big Data Is Not Enough

Big data can give us demographic numbers to crunch and analyze (e.g., knowing that 2015 is the year that millennials outnumbered baby boomers in the workplace, which is indeed a critical data point). But we managers know that numbers do not provide the complete picture of useful knowledge for working in a mutually satisfying way with members of any demographic group. And, each of us is more complex than a singular factor such as generation can depict.

As with any diversity and inclusion challenge, we need to dig deeper. We authors decided to listen to millennials themselves. We wanted to learn from what they had to say in the here and now, specifically:

- What was on their minds?
- What was important to them?

...

Priceless Tip #5

Knowledge is not as important as understanding.

...

There is some disagreement in big data circles about the years between which millennials were born. Some say they were born between 1979-1995. Others say the range is 1982-1994. And some claim the range is 1984-1996.

For our purposes, questioning those who have been on the job for at least a few years made the most sense, so we chose a sample group born 1980-1992. This age span allowed us to compare the older millennials (born 1980-1985) with their younger peers (born 1986-1992).

Our research project was not designed to be academically rigorous, as we were searching for anecdotal themes that could assist managers. However, it was crucial to us to have ample representation across age, sex, region, race, and ethnic lines. Toward this end we worked carefully to ensure our sample group was as inclusive as possible. We realized that folks who choose to take surveys were self-selecting and wondered if our research would produce different information to that of big data research. Together with my brilliant coauthors, we set off on a journey of discovery.

We developed a series of open-ended survey questions and posted them in an online portal. Our original thought was that responses from a small but stratified sample of fifty millennial employees would provide us sufficient real-life insight from which to assist managers.

We launched a social medial campaign to find survey takers. We posted survey invitations and ads on popular social media sites such as Twitter, Facebook, and Pinterest. I also asked for help sourcing respondents from my network on LinkedIn. Surprisingly, in slightly over three months we achieved a respondent pool of over sixty millennial employees, after which we closed the online survey.

For the next eighteen months, I continued to informally collect responses to our six questions from millennial employees I met during business travel to different regions of the US, collecting stories and listening for variances in answers. Beyond the online survey, I spoke to over forty millennial employees.

We distilled the online survey and my extemporaneous conversations down to a final stratified sample of one hundred millennial employees, twice as many as we originally intended. From their responses we searched for themes. Later we examined the responses not used in the stratified sample, looking for additional pertinent comments to illustrate topics. Despite intentionally conducting practical rather than scientific research, we are confident with the face validity of our results.

...

The Millennial Employee Satisfaction Survey©

In our survey we included the usual demographic questions and asked respondents to answer six open-ended core questions, encouraging them to add specific examples where possible:

1. What 2-3 things do you need from your work environment to be most engaged and productive?

2. What 2-3 elements have to be in place for you to be willing to stay with your employer?

3. What 2-3 things would make you want to leave your employer?

4. What 2-3 things would inspire you to work beyond your typical workday (i.e., overtime)?

5. What are your long-term career goals? How about your long-term personal goals?

6. When I am in a professional position of leadership, I imagine the work culture I create will have the following elements…

When we started the project we had no idea how our survey participants would respond. Therefore, only after the surveys were completed and the responses were carefully interpreted did we know what we were going to write about. Only then could we provide practical assistance to managers and create our "Priceless Tips For Managers."

After the formal response collection phase was completed, and we created our stratified sample, we sorted and classified keywords, making sure the most frequently mentioned themes became topics for additional research and writing. We also decided that it made sense for millennial coauthors Amanda and Nikie to analyze and interpret what the hundreds of answers to the open-ended questions actually meant to their contemporaries.

…

Priceless Tip #6

Millennial employees belong to a truly different subculture than their older managers. Be prepared to shift gears to accommodate these cultural differences.

…

Shortly after the data analysis phase, Nikie, who had recently married, also relocated to another state and began working a new job. Subsequently, she found she did not have the bandwidth to continue with the project. I hated losing her as a collaborator but I knew her decision made sense. She contributed to the research analysis and chapter structure, wrote her comments in one chapter, and then bid adieu to the project.

Amanda and I also slowed down our chapter writing rhythm to meet her needs. She too was newly married and had launched her marketing company shortly after we began writing. Knowing that tips about being an effective manager are valuable however and whenever we managers receive them, I took my cues from her. I adjusted my expectations to meet the full range of goals in each of our lives, not just my inherent need to achieve results at lightening speed.

What follows is a synthesis of the perspectives of the employees who took our survey, the insight of this veteran manager (Malati), and my coauthor and millennial cultural informant (Amanda). For managers, the value gained from reading the employee accounts and Priceless Tips will help you create an energetic, engaging workplace. It will enable your team's culture to be one where all employees are enjoying doing their best work and thriving harmoniously together.

...

Priceless Tip #7

In order to build a workplace culture in which everyone can thrive, respect the "rules for survival and success" of your employees.

...

In this book we have included actual survey responses to our open-ended questions. We guaranteed confidentiality and anonymity to all survey respondents. To meet this commitment we have occasionally edited comments so respondents would not be easily identifiable. As best we could, we have retained the responses verbatim, as the manner in which respondents wrote their answers often gave us much insight into their meaning.

You will note that in the following chapters Amanda provides her personal narrative, demonstrating how the themes we detected in our research have impacted her directly.

We have also included examples of managers who developed successful tactics for achieving their goals while working with millennial employees. For the few who asked not to be identified, we provide fictitious names and changed their locations and industries.

Although we hold the copyright to The Millennial Employee Satisfaction Survey©, one of our guiding principles is that we are all in this work of managing and leading others together. If you would like to use this survey at your organization, or within your work group, please send us an email for permission.

...

Chapter Two Bonus Exercise

Managers on multiple continents are facing the same challenges you are. As they develop and share practices that work with us, we will pass them along in social media posts or blog articles. Please send us what works for you as well. We would be thrilled to share your success stories too.

... ...

Chapter Three

THE KINDERGARTEN SYNDROME

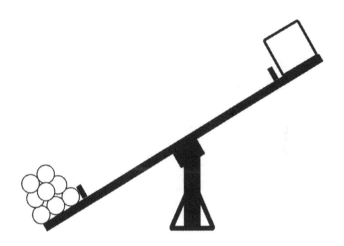

As we combed through the survey data looking for major common threads, we focused on the trends that came from the surveys alone, rather than be influenced by others' definitions of millennials.

One element our respondents repeatedly mentioned which motivated and retained them was a sense of fairness and equality in the workplace. This is not surprising, considering how the tremendous advances made during the American Civil Rights

Movement and the Women's Liberation Movement heavily influenced the lives of their parents. These movements raised consciousness and championed for equal rights, reducing many legislative and social barriers based on race and sex, thereby challenging the status quo of white male advantage. Being reared by parents and teachers who may have supported these battles or who may have benefitted from the achievements of this era would quite naturally influence employees to expect something different from their personal and work lives as adults.

...

"Everyone deserves to have an equal opportunity to succeed. So I guess that the employees who demonstrated the right combination of being the smartest, accomplishing the most, and working the hardest, may deserve to be farther ahead on the promotion ladder and gain more than those of us with less stellar performance."

...

"I would leave my employer if they treated me unfairly in any capacity. If there was discrimination within the work environment then I would leave as well."

...

Equal opportunity for all to succeed is a perennial consideration in American society. It is at the root of the all-American spirit to "pull yourself up by your bootstraps" and elevate your position regardless of your background, fighting against societal forces such as discrimination and micro-inequities. Striving to attain legal and social equality for oppressed groups continues to be an essential challenge for US communities and employers alike. Indeed, many millennials are reflecting the values their parents fought for. To many of our young respondents, the importance of fairness extended beyond individual success and their workplace peers to the world at large. We found that their commitment to end discrimination and create a fair and just society was a strong call to action.

•••

"What if we are the generation to change this mentality?"

•••

"What if we create a movement and take a stand for real equality?"

•••

For numerous millennials, however, these egalitarian values have taken a step beyond creating opportunity for those who were historically prevented from success. For some respondents, "equality" meant something different than earlier social movements or laws defined it or how we enforce the laws through agencies such as the US Department of Labor or the Equal Employment Opportunity Commission. The concept of equality was often interpreted as *identical* treatment, regardless of seniority, experience, or merit-based factors.

...

<u>Priceless Tip #8</u>

Do not assume you understand the meaning of what your employee is saying just because you are both using the same words in the same language.

...

Much like the administrative assistant I spoke of in the first chapter, many of our respondents wanted to discard factors that they perceived to negatively influence their work or personal lives, but may actually be important to the overall health of the organization. Their concepts of fairness and equality were centered on opportunities for personal advancement or benefit.

...

> *"My boss gives the agent sitting closest to her more information than she gives me. I'm worried that's going to put this agent in a better position for a promotion than me."*

...

> *"My family lived four hours' drive away from me. I never had the opportunity to see them because the older employees always chose the best holidays for their long weekends. It was most irritating because I felt I was surpassing them in speed, accuracy, and production."*

...

...

"I'd stay with this company if there was an equal opportunity for me and all workers capable of outstanding work to have equal assignments."

...

Standing up for equality, albeit sometimes a simplified interpretation of parity, was a major trend in what we heard. Though most respondents held strong opinions about equal opportunity in the work environment, these sentiments appeared linked to their days as children, where everyone was treated as remarkable, and received frequent accolades for their performance.

...

"I need to feel appreciated. I like to be recognized for my efforts."

...

One variance we noted, however, was that this crucial millennial value was somewhat divided along the age-or-stage continuum. Our older group of respondents (born 1980-1985) who had already reached a level of achievement in their careers demonstrated a stronger inner realist, reminding them that even such idealistic concepts could be taken too far, and a reaction to a perceived slight could land one out of work. Very few of the younger group (born 1986-1992) expressed that insight or concern:

...

"I'd leave my employer if there was no appreciation for the hard work I've put in. I'd have no incentive to work any harder and see any more success."

...

Millennials' expectation of identical treatment, whereby traditional hierarchical values may carry less weight, is what we have termed the "Kindergarten Syndrome." As we considered this further, millennial coauthor Amanda shared a time in her career where similar thoughts and feelings emerged.

...

Amanda's Kindergarten Syndrome Experience

It was in my first full-time professional position that I recall feeling slighted, and I honestly wanted to stomp home and complain like a kindergarten-aged child, "this isn't fair!" I was working for a small company that acted as a marketing resource for a larger group of businesses. The company was structured into two marketing arms. One covered communication outreach efforts and media relations, the other focused on direct-to-consumer promotions by producing events throughout the year. Each branch was comprised of a manager who answered directly to the executive director and a coordinator who supported that manager. I was working as the coordinator within the consumer promotions branch.

I shared a workspace, or "bullpen" as we called it, with the other coordinator who had come onboard about eighteen months prior to me. While she was my senior in terms of tenure with the company, I had more experience working in the industry and had been involved with the company as a volunteer for many years.

The leadership of this organization wisely made sure to constantly provide opportunities for us both to grow professionally. After just over a year I excelled in my position and demonstrated the ability to take on new responsibilities. My fellow coordinator colleague had also evolved in some ways as well. But, with only seven total employees, there wasn't a lot of upward growth opportunity. But we understood that the evolution of our existing positions provided us the experience to grow professionally.

One day we were all called in to the executive director's office to celebrate the promotion of the manager of the communications outreach branch to a newly created director position. Simultaneously, the other coordinator had been promoted to manager. While the competitive side of my nature drove me to want more for myself, I understood that she had been there longer and thus the timing wasn't right for me. In that moment I started to understand the role that seniority played.

Six months later, I was in the process of wrapping up a very aggressive events season, making huge strides over the quality and quantity of work I had accomplished the prior season. I had quantifiable results to demonstrate my progress. In a conversation with the executive director about my future plans and what I would need from the organization, I mentioned that while the focus on promotion may seem frivolous to her, I felt I had performed at a level that deserved recognition and a promotion matching that of my colleague.

Although the conversation that evening covered many areas of looking forward, what stood out to me most was her reaction to my request. She said that she was hesitant to give me the promotion because the coordinator she previously promoted had more time on the job than me and viewed herself as more skilled. My promotion would present "challenges" to the director.

It was in this moment that I confronted the concept of creating an equal workplace. To please the other millennial employee, a position was created to fill her need for outward recognition. However, that created a situation in which another employee (me) was held back. Seniority was cited as the reason but in my mind it was irrelevant as we worked in different branches of the organization.

Suddenly I felt slighted. I believed in the mission of the organization to the degree that I was willing to work tremendously long hours and achieve superb results. I expected to be recognized by the organization via a promotion to the next level. It felt like they did not have the same belief in me. The organization valued the other employee over me and was not willing to upset her.

Looking back on that experience and reviewing the findings of our research, I realize how important it is to our generation that everyone has equal chances to succeed. If we feel that is not the case, or there is a lack of fairness, we would not hesitate to leave an employer. That is exactly what I did.

...

A Case Study In Managing The Kindergarten Syndrome

John Schnetzler owns Keoni's Property Services, a residential renovation and remodeling company in Hawai'i. Most of his employees were born in the millennial generation years. When he promoted one employee to foreman he started noticing an undercurrent of complaining: "that's not fair."

He quickly made up informal promotional "titles" for each of his employees, based on individual interests: "Wizard," "Ninja," and "Super Woman." He then purchased new company t-shirts sporting each employee's new "title."

Almost like magic, the young employees were happy again. All was fair in their world. When the older staff received their t-shirts with titles such as "Maestro" and "Duke," they laughed, suggesting to John that he was slightly nuts. Still, they went along with the program with good humor and accepted their new monikers.

...

Priceless Tip #9

Millennials, especially the younger ones, need more "Gold Stars" than older employees. Give them out generously, even if it is just for their hard work.

...

Priceless Tip #10

Anticipate in advance that good news for one employee may not feel like good news for another employee.

...

Perception is reality. Whether or not the millennial employees' demand for equality seems extreme is not the issue. Employees need to know in advance and continually be reminded that some decisions are going to be made that do not seem fair.

Acknowledge your superstar performers as soon as you can via some outward means that suits that individual's style and needs: a promotion, a pay raise, a bonus day off, or something more creative.

...

Priceless Tip #11

Before giving an employee public recognition, make sure you know it will be welcomed by the employee and not be a source of embarrassment.

...

"I like compliments and words of affirmation so I know when I'm doing a good job."

...

"I'm talented and fast. I want to feel like my work is valued at the firm and appreciated by my manager."

...

As mentioned earlier, writing this book has been a multiple-year journey. The initially frustrating starts and stops ultimately provided us longer-term insight into the topic and our subjects. Some older members of the generation are now reaching the milestones typically identified as full adulthood: a history of working in several organizations, establishing their career paths and getting promotions into higher levels of responsibility, developing a level of authority in their field, and getting married and having children. Along with maturation, comes a diminished need for Gold Stars.

You might find however, that using your older millennials as thought partners will provide unique benefits for you, them, your work unit, and your organization.

...

Chapter Three Bonus Exercise

Create an informal spreadsheet with the name of each employee in column A. In column B, indicate what you think each employee's personalized Gold Star might be.

... ...

Chapter Four

WHAT DO WE WANT TO BE WHEN WE GROW UP? CAREER DEVELOPMENT

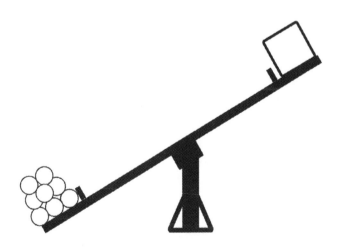

Companies enthusiastically brand how wonderfully they treat their employees, whether they actually do or not. Human resources departments are now called "People Resources," "People Champions," or "People and Culture." Employees are referred to as "Team Members," "Associates," or "Partners." Company website career pages show stock photos of happy millennial faces in order to attract more happy millennial faces.

As millennials outnumber all other generations in the workplace, and leave organizations more easily than any other generation, satisfying what they need is as mission-critical a priority as gaining and retaining customer market share. Remembering that the human brain is not fully mature until around age twenty-five, a more mature (read: older) manager has a critical role in the growth and development of his/her millennials, not just as employees but also as developing adults.

...

Priceless Tip #12

Accept it. You have an important role to play
in your millennial employees' lives.

...

Priceless Tip #13

Take each of your staff members out for lunch once
in a while. It does not have to be fancy or expensive.
It just needs to be dedicated one-on-one time.

...

Employees of all ages need to see that their managers have their best interests in mind, even if the larger organization does so only nominally. For many millennials, a close and authentic interpersonal connection with their manager is more essential than it was for many employees in previous generations.

•••

*"I feel like I can tell my manager anything. All my
friends are so jealous that I have such a great boss."*

•••

As latchkey children they were often left alone and they led
highly structured lives, with carpools chauffeuring them from
one activity, practice, or lesson to the next. They developed
problem-solving tactics early in life and learned to negotiate
the world at a young age. Therefore, many millennials grew
up as simultaneously self-sufficient and highly regulated by the
adults in their lives.

The parenting philosophy of "quality over quantity" was a
truism for many millennials when they were children. While
parents may have needed to be at work when the children
came home from school, they were often highly involved in
their children's emotional lives. These baby boomer parents
openly discussed topics their parents would have avoided even
alluding to. Many spoke transparently with their children about
topics that were previously considered adult-only, such as sex,
politics, war, economics, the environment, and perhaps even
why mommy and daddy were not going to be living together
anymore. During these conversations, the children's thoughts
and feelings were acknowledged and valued. They also brought
their kids to the job site on "Bring Your Child To Work Day."
Sometimes, if the parents were under deadline, children went
to work with them on the weekend.

Every generation's patterns in childhood influence how
members of that generation think, feel, and behave as adults.
Millennials' close emotional and working relationship with

elders from a young age naturally leads to the following sentiment, which was echoed amongst our respondents:

...

"The workplace needs to feel like a second home."

...

So what is it like at home? Here are a few descriptions of what makes work feel like home:

...

"I need good music to keep me upbeat. And, I need a friendly atmosphere. The more positive the atmosphere, the harder I work to keep up the good work."

...

"We all need a fun and welcoming environment, one that is supportive and open to our continued growth."

...

"I like to be comfortable and happy where I work."

...

"The other day, my president walked by my computer and I was playing a club song, "Bulletproof," by La Roux. The president got all excited and had me blast it. Apparently we both like that song. And the rest of

the office couldn't help but smile and enjoy the music
as well."

...

Priceless Tip #14

As each work group is unique, develop ways to create an atmosphere of connection for your particular group.

...

Another aspect of a typical millennial childhood was parents who continued to be highly involved when their children went to college, the military, or trade school. Parents enthusiastically helped their millennial kids sort out the process of choosing their direction. Many actively assisted with every step of the entry process into adulthood.

It should be no surprise that millennial employees anticipate something similar from their managers. Having regular conversations with their managers about their current role and their future is important to them. Managers can expect their role to include helping their youngest employees sort through career options.

...

Priceless Tip #15

Show each employee that you care about his/ her future, however s/he defines it.

...

When asked about longer-term goals, the responses were surprisingly typical for workers of most generations when they were starting careers:

●●●

"I'm not as totally sure about work goals as I am about personal goals: I'd like to buy my own house by the time I am 25 and get married."

●●●

"Work-wise I have goals to move out of a customer-facing role, maybe into compliance or something."

●●●

"Personally, I would like to have my own place and a puppy. Seems silly, but yeah."

●●●

We are not suggesting you need to go out and buy your staff member a puppy, kitten, or pet python. You do need to know what is important to them though. If your employees are willing to tell strangers (us) about cherished details of their personal lives in a survey, they would probably be thrilled to share the same with you, their manager. If it is important to them, it needs to be important to you.

...

"I need clear steps for my advancement. It must be laid out so I can actively measure my progress toward achieving a set goal over time."

...

Priceless Tip #16

Be an active career counselor to your millennial employees. And, share your own career journey. Perhaps they can avoid some of the mistakes you've made.

...

One of our respondents graduated from college and worked for a large global consulting firm for several years. For many older employees, just working at this elite organization would be seen as triumphant in and of itself. But despite the standard job rotations and advanced educational opportunities provided to high potential employees, he was unenthusiastic, minimally engaged at work, and was considering leaving the company. His reason: he was unable to envision his future career path and was bored moving from one division to another with no end in sight.

Although the company had successfully groomed tens of thousands of employees using this role rotation formula, it may not be enough for those in this generation with high potential. Another respondent presented this dilemma quite poignantly:

...

"Sure, I need positive reinforcement and need to feel appreciated. But, I don't have a dream to chase. I'm

just miserable. They motivate me to get out of bed in the morning and work toward an abundant future but that's all."

...

"If an employer can help me beyond the quiet desperation of mere survival and teach me to dream, then help me to fulfill those dreams, then I will be actively engaged and working toward making my dreams come true."

...

By listening deeply to the emotional needs behind these statements, we may find a simple solution to the problem facing the big consulting firm. It may not need to scrap its high potential fast-track program and start from scratch. Perhaps it needs to increase each manager's ability to converse with their millennial employees about what is important to them, including their short- and long-term life goals. Helping the young employees connect the dots so they can see how they are progressing toward achieving their personal career goals – their dreams – is a welcome and needed gift a willing manager can provide.

...

Priceless Tip #17

Upgrade your consulting skills so you can be a supportive manager. Learn about your millennial employees' short- and long-term goals.

...

As we saw earlier, employees who had supportive parents and teachers expect supportive managers when they are in the workplace. Not surprisingly, the concept of "support" was one of the most frequently mentioned topics amongst our respondents.

...

"I like doing a good job at work and I need my manager to be supportive that, right now, I'm not looking to build my long-term career. I'm saving up money so I can quit and be home with kids."

...

"If I was in a leadership role, I would create a supportive work environment that encourages creativity as well as personal development."

...

"When the management team expresses interest in supporting my career and my goals, it motivates me to also spend time exploring what I want and how to get there."

...

Professional consultants, human resources business partners, learning and organizational development specialists, and sales employees must know how to determine their clients' needs by asking probing questions. Their success depends on this skill. Managers of people, especially managers of millennial employees, require the same level of aptitude in consultative listening and asking probing questions.

...

Priceless Tip #18

Start career conversations by asking
questions such as, "If you could do anything
in the world, what would it be?"

...

Priceless Tip #19

Help your employees achieve their dreams. Work with
them to set up a clear development path that will get
them to where they want to go. And, introduce them
to your professional network to help expand theirs.

...

*"I would consider leaving my employer if I felt the
barriers to achievement were too great."*

...

*"I need a boss who gives feedback and opportunities
to attend courses, conferences, seminars, etc. for my
continuing education."*

...

*"I just realized that the glass ceiling is inches above
my head. I came here to learn and become an active
partner in this company but I can see it's not going
to happen. I'm now planning how I'm going to get
out of here."*

...

Noticeably absent in our survey responses were statements indicating that our respondents saw how they fit into the big picture of the organization in which they worked.

Employees of all ages view their organization through the myopic lens of "my work group." They often do not know what is going on beyond their work unit and have even less understanding about how their role fits into the greater picture of the organization's vision, mission, and goals. This is not atypical, but it is something you can change that may help your millennial employees as well as your organization's retention rates.

...

Priceless Tip #20

Tie it together for them. Discuss how your employees' current roles and next steps fit into their career goals, your department's goals, and the organization's big-picture goals.

...

Priceless Tip #21

Insert "Career Goals" on the agenda of a work-group meeting occasionally. By encouraging open dialogue about mid- and long-term goals, members of your work group can become resources for each other. It's also a great move toward building a cohesive team.

...

···

Amanda's Experience: What's In A Title?

While we don't always admit to it, the cold hard fact is that we millennials are the children of the professional world. We hate to admit this fact because, thanks to that Kindergarten Syndrome, we want to be treated the same as our long-tenured colleagues. In conversations with my peers and in our survey responses, the answers to the questions "What are long-term career goals?" and "How about your long-term personal goals?" had a pattern of response that only minimally surprised me about my age-mates.

I've read in articles over and over again that one thing that's challenging about this new group of people in the workforce is our emphasis on titles. Looking to this I recognize the effect that titles have had on my own experiences.

Some companies have created new, casual, fun, and edgy work environments to brand themselves as the employer of choice. They work to create titles that attract the types of personalities that will thrive in their setting. Titles are being created to fit a particular employee who can succeed in the new game-changing environment. Unique titles such as "Public Happy Maker," "Web Alchemist," "Conjurer of Communications," and "Word-of-Mouth Marketer" were designed specifically for millennial employees. The demeaning "entry-level position" is now avoided through creativity.

Personally, thinking back to the Kindergarten Syndrome I experienced in Chapter Three, at the root of my challenge was the issue of not being given a fair and equal chance to advance to a new title based on merit, simply because that advancement might make a colleague feel badly.

While the overall issue was tied to my sense of fairness, the specific detail that bothered me was that the other colleague received the coveted title "manager" while I was stuck with "coordinator." It was at this very point in my career that *title* suddenly became critically important. One factor that subconsciously swayed my decision to leave this employer and work for another company was my need for a title, an obvious indicator of my career path.

This was also later apparent in two specific scenarios. The first occasion was my salary negotiation meeting with the new company's president and the CFO/human resources manager. Although it wasn't obvious to me, the CFO was silently focused on the benefits package she was negotiating as we discussed the role I would play in the position they were creating for me.

She slid a piece of paper across the table to the president with the word "manager" circled. Fresh off the heels of being told by my previous employer that this was a title that I couldn't have, the status of being at the management level suddenly had greater importance to me than it had coming into the negotiation.

The second occasion was my first actual workday. Coming into a newly created position meant the opportunity to develop it. One of my very first tasks was to determine what my specific title would be. I considered numerous options, which I then sent to the people I respected most in my professional life. It took nearly ten days of agonizing over the choice before finally selecting a title. The funny thing is that while I considered some off-the-wall options inspired by the edgy companies that started this trend, I decided on "Business Integration Manager." In my mind it wasn't the boring old "Marketing Manager" or "Business Development" title, but it brought both together in a manner conservative enough that, I hoped, would help me appear older and further along in my career than I actually was. Given the perfect opportunity to build a title that fit me, I chose a title that I wanted to grow into.

Looking back today I would love to say that I've matured in my career and having a title no longer means anything, that I only care about the quality of the work I do. But that wouldn't be honest at all. Having matured in my career, however, I don't look at a title as restricting what I can do or defining the expectations of what I need to become.

...

Chapter Four Bonus Exercise

Ask your employees to give themselves titles that reflect their future selves: a role they may hold sometime in their career or family life in the future. Then invite them to print and post their new titles in/on their workspace or uniform. Malati has decided her new title would be: *Maven For Managers of Millennials*

... ...

Chapter Five

YEAH TEAM! THE WORK ENVIRONMENT

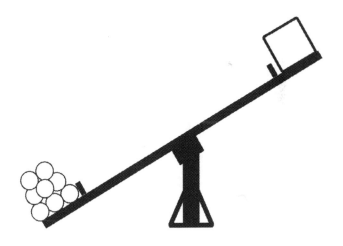

A cornerstone element of most elementary education programs for today's millennials was learning based on collaboration and cooperation rather than competition. Seeing children in small clusters working out math problems or reading aloud together was more the norm than it had been for previous generations where each child was expected to achieve entirely independent of classmates. New cooperative games were developed for the playground and classroom.

By high school, students were often graded based on the results of their group project's success, in addition to individual contribution. Teachers gave specific goals and due dates with broad guidelines, but project groups often needed to develop their own objectives, roles, and tactical plans to achieve these goals.

Colleges and trade schools often use these same methodologies. Indeed, many top-rated medical schools, such as UCLA's David Geffen School of Medicine, assemble first-year medical students into cohorts for problem-based learning. The military has always provided group-based learning, as it relies on individuals as well as the cohesion of the unit to achieve goals.

As we have seen in previous chapters, the logical progression of these pedagogical approaches is teamwork as a high priority in the work environment. We heard this theme from respondents across all demographics. Working within a team and the positive influence of the team environment was a high priority to those surveyed. Very few employees stated that a solitary work environment motivated them:

...

"I prefer environments where organizations work as a team."

...

"Most people like to feel like part of a team rather than just being told what to do."

...

...

"I am energized and thrive with human interaction. Even though I work in a cubicle-like environment, friendships are encouraged amongst employees."

...

Priceless Tip #22

Expect many of your younger employees to want to work together more often than to work as individual contributors.

...

Priceless Tip #23

Create small project teams whenever you see the opportunity.

...

When we realize that most of our millennial workers are only years out from their college or military service, and as a group tend to postpone marriage and children, we see the importance for them of forging friendships with coworkers.

...

"I enjoy casual relationships with coworkers; people who get along outside work will succeed inside work."

...

...

"I love working with fun, driven people! They create a cool culture. People who can laugh, handle their stress well, and still work their butts off."

...

Priceless Tip #24

Learn to be more tolerant of what your generation may have considered "immature" behavior in the workplace.

...

The Crowd Boos!

What is the flip side of being a more tolerant manager? We saw from the survey that the risk in the workplace is the same as any collegiate project group: frustration if one member of the group does not come through for the "good of the team." Here is the caveat:

...

"As long as both parties understand the importance of getting the job done, a casual relationship should help the work environment."

...

"I've been in situations where a coworker isn't completely fulfilling their role and that means additional

work for me. Worse yet is when the company doesn't address it!"

...

"I so need better-trained coworkers."

...

Changing Teams

If you have read the professional literature on retention, or why employees leave jobs, you know that the top two reasons employees stay or leave revolve around the work environment.

To our question, "What 2-3 things would make you want to leave your employer?" most responses were variations of the themes of negative coworkers or negative bosses:

...

"Aggressive coworkers"

...

"Negative colleagues"

...

"Cliques and groups in the workplace causing drama"

...

One of our older respondents was very clear about managerial conduct that would motivate her to leave:

"Companies must pick and choose their battles, but some consistently don't deal with things. The company would have to make some courageous/unpleasant decisions. Sometimes that choice is not made because it seems too difficult."

...

Priceless Tip #25

As much as you may hate confrontation, managing the behavior of your staff and holding employees accountable for how they act is critical for developing an enjoyable, tension-free, and productive environment.

...

Priceless Tip #26

Pay attention to undercurrents of dissatisfaction or active disengagement amongst members of project teams. If you sense something is off, or if someone complains about another team member, immediately address the situation. The following tip has nine steps you can use to assist an employee to improve his/her behavior.

...

Priceless Tip #27

Employ these nine steps to coach employees who need to improve their behavior:

1. Describe the employee's negative behavior.
2. Describe the impact the behavior has on the group's ability to achieve its goals.
3. Ask the employee to provide 1-2 viable solutions toward correcting the behavior, then add your own ideas.
4. Explain to the employee what may happen next if s/he does not correct the behavior.
5. Make sure you have a verbal indication that your employee understands the importance of the changes needed and is willing to make those changes.
6. Set a schedule to touch base and review progress once each week, or more frequently if necessary.
7. Follow up with an email detailing all elements of the conversation.
8. Keep your commitment to meet with the employee as scheduled.
9. Give the employee kudos for small wins as s/he develops the more positive behavior.

...

Yes, this process is demanding, uncomfortable, and time-consuming. But being a manager means managing people as much as it means managing projects. The rewards of a more pleasant work environment are higher productivity and greater retention. Following these coaching steps is well worth the effort.

Ok, you think...perform these same nine performance management steps with each negative employee and that should take care of the negative work environment situation. Nope, sorry, there is one even more important element that creates an unsatisfactory workplace.

The second reason that emerged in the question regarding reasons an employee would quit is: the negative boss!

A negative manager can pollute a work environment faster than a negative team member. Managers will find their millennial employees running for the door if they are perceived as:

...

"A negative manager"

...

"A micromanager"
or
"A verbally abusive boss"

...

Priceless Tip #28

If you have ever been given feedback that you micromanage or are a boss who is difficult to get along with, improve your interpersonal and people-management skills immediately through learning and practice. And, get a coach to assist you in gaining mastery of your new skills faster.

...

Why is this so critical? As most employees view their company narrowly rather than broadly, their manager or their manager's manager is the what/who they are referring to when speaking about "the company." To your employees, their friends, their social media friends, and their friends' networks of friends, the company is a horrible place to work if you are a horrible person to work for.

No one wants to work for a micromanaging or verbally abusive boss. Millennial employees may or may not tell you what they think of your people management skills. They will, however, quit – and tell everyone they know why.

So look at this low tolerance for negativity as a professional development opportunity.

...

Priceless Tip #29

If you have not had the opportunity to experience a 360-degree multi-rater feedback process, find a valid and reliable feedback tool and have your boss, colleagues, and direct reports provide you feedback. If you have previously obtained 360-degree feedback, conduct the survey again with your current team.

...

It is not enough to get feedback from your team, especially your millennial team members, who often grew up with open adult dialogues with their parents. You need to share the results, or at least what you learned from the feedback. All your employees deserve that courtesy and your millennial employees expect it from you! By sharing what you learn from the feedback with your team you can also elicit actions you might take to improve. As my mother used to say, "What's good for the goose is good for the gander." Translated into performance management parlance: whatever you expect of your employees they will also expect of you.

...

Malati's First Multi-Rater Feedback Experience

I know from personal experience how challenging this process may be, as over the years I have periodically asked my teams to provide me feedback. I used Kouzes and Posner's Leadership Practices Inventory® (LPI®) because I wanted to explore evidence-based, learnable behaviors, not how warm and fuzzy I was. I had used this tool for many groups and saw hundreds of managers grow and improve their behaviors as a result of using the LPI®.

I held a pretty high opinion of myself as an effective manager and leader of people, so I was more than surprised when the LPI® report I distributed to bosses, peers, and members of my team showed me lacking in in a few specific behaviors! My scores weren't egregious; they were just out of synch with my perception of myself, particularly around the cluster of behaviors that demonstrate the frequency at which I took action based on my team members' suggestions. Yikes!

I knew my bosses would provide me honest feedback and chose peers who would do the same. But I was worried that my team might be reticent. After all, who wants to tell the boss that she doesn't utilize enough of the suggestions she claims she wants?

Before giving my team members the LPI®, I promised I would share the results of the feedback they gave me. I kept my word and presented it to them: "Here's your manager Malati, warts and all." I was fortunate that my team took their feedback as seriously as I did. Together we set a few behavior goals and milestones for me. I then set out to improve my skills as a manager of people.

A benefit of being transparent was my team's good-natured commitment to help keep me on track (read: pointing out when I was off track). It was not always comfortable for me, but it certainly sped up my professional development! Also, it built a foundation upon which I could then assist them in the development of their professional behavior. By the time I met my millennial Nikie, who inspired this book (see Chapter One), I was skilled enough to build an authentic, mutually beneficial relationship with an employee. I also learned how to conduct group suggestion meetings and inform the team of the reasoning behind my choosing one route or a hybrid of suggested routes they provided, or why I did not utilize their suggestions.

If it were not for me taking on this challenge earlier in my career, I am not sure I would have been aware of my need to learn those skills. By asking and sharing my LPI® feedback and then soliciting additional behavior change ideas from that initial team I was able to expedite my growth as a caring and competent manager.

...

Priceless Tip #30

Establish an accountability partnership with another manager and use peer-to-peer coaching to improve whatever behaviors you may be exhibiting that would give your low-tolerance millennial employees reason to leave.

...

<u>Chapter Five Bonus Exercise</u>

Interview an intercollegiate athletic coach to learn ways to create a cohesive team atmosphere.

... ...

Chapter Six

GROWING UP IN A DIGITAL WORLD: COMMUNICATION AND FLEXIBILITY

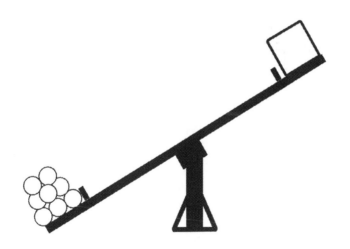

Amanda's Digital Native Experience

"Digital natives" and "digital immigrants." The first time I had an employer use this terminology in talking about our generation, I was sitting across from the other new hire that joined the company the same day I did. The company president was introducing us to the management team as its two newest members. She described how I was the youngest at the management level and how I would be working in company marketing and business development to rebrand and strategize the company's products and services. The president expressed specific excitement about me being a "digital native."

I'm sure this was meant as a compliment. Somehow, though, the comment didn't sit right with me. It is accurate to a degree, as I enjoy technology and enjoy the opportunity to integrate it in ways that can simplify our lives. However, for my entire life I've been surrounded by peers that I'm confident far outpace me in digital thinking and ability. I may be above average in competence but I'm certainly not at the very top.

But this fact wasn't what made the statement feel wrong. The president then turned to introduce the other new member to the team member. He was about fifteen years older than me, a member of Generation X. He was introduced as a "digital immigrant" to further qualify the "digital native" designation given to me.

I was instantly embarrassed. True, the other new hire technically wasn't born into a digital world but he had chosen to keep up with it and outpaced my digital skills to such a degree that I was embarrassed to even be compared to him, let alone have it implied that I was somehow superior to him as a "native." He once hacked his friend's computers as a joke and wrote his own computer programs. If there was a problem, he could find software to customize – problem solved. I was nowhere near the same level of digital competence. I had been placed in a box based on the year I was born, not based on my actual skill.

...

Priceless Tip #31

"We millennials don't want to be placed into situations based on what you think you know about us." - Amanda

...

The digital influence on millennials is tremendous but keep in mind it's not our knowledge of technology but the fact that we never knew a world without technology that makes us different from older generations.

Our expertise with high levels of technology will vary just as it does with people from all generations. However, when we approach problems, we've always been able to consider technology as one of the tools to arrive at solutions. We thus continue to approach the challenges of the workplace keeping these tools front of mind.

...

Priceless Tip #32

In addition to the obvious caution of not stereotyping all millennial employees as having any single characteristic, remember that each one is a unique person first.

...

...

Flexible Scheduling: Amanda's Experience

As I read through the responses of my peers, there were a few trends tied closely to our comfort with technology. Our office has never stopped at the door. With cell phones, video calling, international calling, emailing, text messaging/instant messaging, and social media – just to name a few – we've never felt out of touch. To unplug in our world means you may shut down your computer but you always keep one eye out for a push notification from your phone.

The argument of how healthy all this communication is or isn't will be debated for some time, I'm sure. But our generation doesn't know any different way of being. With this feeling of always being on call, however, we ask for something back: flexible schedules.

I've always been a "work hard so you can play hard" personality. I push myself beyond the forty-hour work week because I know it allows me to indulge in the activities that drive me to get out of bed each day besides work. For me, the main activity is horseback riding. In college, I grouped my classes in the morning or afternoon, and since student activities most often were held in the evenings, I could easily find up to thirty hours of daylight hours each week to enjoy time at the barn.

I knew that in my first job in the "real world" I would be scaling back my riding time, but I still expected to dedicate two hours per trip to the barn during a few mid-week days. When I started the job in June, it wasn't a problem. As the winter days became shorter, I realized the flexible routine I had become accustomed to the previous four years at college was very different than my Monday through Friday, 8am to 5pm workdays now allowed.

I met with my manager to see what solutions existed, and she seemed to have a difficult time understanding my need to fit this into my schedule. Knowing myself and what was important to producing my best quality work, I continued pushing. I went above my manager to the director, who regularly spoke of the importance of each employee engaging in whatever was needed to produce his/her best work.

With pressure from the director we were able to find a solution: on agreed-upon days I would come in an hour early so that I could leave at 4:00 pm with enough daylight to sneak in a ride. My manager abided by the change as she was asked to by the director. But it was also clear that she didn't appreciate the change in routine.

On the days that my schedule flexed to allow me to ride, her communication, support, and guidance with me seemed most challenging. I didn't mind regularly returning to the office at 6:00 pm to squeeze in more work for the day that I might not have finished before I left at 6:00 pm. I did mind that in small ways I was being made to feel uncomfortable for standing up for what I knew I needed to do to make me the best employee I could be. Eventually the pressure wore on me until I realized this position was not one I could continue in for the long term.

...

Malati's Reaction Upon First Reading Amanda's Account

Whoa, Nelly! She went over her manager's head when she did not get her way?!

It is my educated guess that being commanded by the director to acquiesce to the needs of this barely-graduated-from-college employee had far greater influence on the manager's subsequent attitude regarding flexibility than Amanda's need to leave at 4:00 pm and return at 6:00 pm to finish her work.

I am pretty sure I would not have liked my employee "jumping over me" either. However, I would respond by being more direct. After grousing about it at home, I would probably approach the boss-jumping employee and explain that I would have preferred if she came directly to me to work out our issues. That is how professionals (read: adults in my generation) manage conflict. Further, I would tell her of my concern that this would set a precedent. A team's ability to meet and exceed its goals with everyone working as a cohesive whole is always my priority. A ground swell of employees running to speak with my boss each time they did not get their way would negatively impact that cohesion.

...

Priceless Tip #33

Establish a strong, honest relationship with your boss. There are a multitude of reasons for this critical relationship, not the least of which is the ability to confer on a sensitive topic before one of your employees does.

...

Priceless Tip #34

Make sure your values are in alignment with your organization's values and expectations. If your company supports flexible work schedules and it is part of the organizational culture, learn how and when it can be beneficial to your team's employee engagement and productivity.

...

Priceless Tip #35

If you sincerely cannot work within your company's values, expectations, and organizational culture, consider changing companies. It will save you a lot of stress and prevent a potential epidemic of staff exits.

...

Priceless Tip #36

Meet with each of your employees to determine each one's flexibility needs. Then be sincere in your attempt to meet these needs. Reasonable employees will appreciate you taking the first step toward meeting their needs and will negotiate something that will not compromise work goals.

...

Flexible Scheduling: Malati's Experience

I am a great supporter of flexible work arrangements and have gone out of my way to challenge the status quo at organizations so that members of my team could meet their family, personal, and work needs.

My first coauthor Nikie and I conducted a proof-of-concept telecommuting arrangement. We would agree on her deliverables and then developed a process for her to document her anticipated work-from-home output. She was then held accountable for the quality and deadlines of these deliverables.

This arrangement came in especially handy when she was planning her wedding, which happened simultaneously with our company's core system software conversion planning. Her wedding event project plan was as complex as our conversion project plan. To make it work, she was making a lot of calls from the office. She was mentally stressed and spent a considerable amount of time talking with wedding vendors, sometimes disrupting the quiet needed by her colleagues.

We planned one to two days each week during which she could work from home and make the myriad calls she needed without disrupting the rest of our team and working groups nearby. As her training delivery calendar was planned out months in advance, we could forecast which weeks would be less intensive for her, which weeks she would be traveling, and which weeks she would be in the planning and instructional development mode. With this predictability, we could also determine the best times for her to work from home.

...

Priceless Tip #37

If your organization does not yet embrace flexible scheduling, take a leadership role in establishing it by conducting a proof-of-concept experiment with a member or two of your team.

...

Priceless Tip #38

Communicating with your employees who are working elsewhere remains important. When they are "on the clock" treat them as you would any on-site employee.

...

Priceless Tip #39

Learn to text. For your millennial employees especially, texting is an efficient way to communicate that guarantees quick answers to your questions.

...

The outcome of my experiment with Nikie was as I anticipated. Her output was of the same high quality I had come to expect from her when she was in the office. And her wedding was as perfectly elegant as a celebrity wedding. Owing to the flexible scheduling, I like to think the wedding was a little less stressful than it could have been.

...

Priceless Tip #40

The key to making flex scheduling successful is true flexibility, in spirit as well as in fact, from both you and the employee. Millennial employees will be going through many life-stage transitions. Working with them to determine flexible work arrangements can strengthen your relationships and their engagement with their jobs.

...

...

A Case Study In Managing Flexible Work Environments

Vani R. is an internal communications manager for a telecom company headquartered in Austin, Texas. Her flexible scheduling story is noteworthy as it demonstrates both the benefits and the challenges of flexible scheduling.

Vani provided her employees the schedule variations they needed, in alignment with the company's values. This included working remotely, working off-commute hours, or working split shifts.

Vani's team consisted of ten members with offices spanning two US time zones (Pacific and Central Time) and one time zone in India. Five of her US employees were older millennials, as was she. She was thirty-three years old when we interviewed her.

As Bangalore, India is 10.5-11.5 hours ahead of Texas and 12.5-13.5 hours ahead of her team in California, the window for meeting during a normal workday on both continents was not easy under any circumstance.

Vani established a standardized weekly team meeting schedule, rotating which location had to be in the office either very early or very late so that they all shared the burden. Not all employees could be at every meeting, so her solution was to make sure everyone had agendas well ahead of time and could provide their input. She also video recorded the meetings so employees could later view the ones they missed and keep up with the team's progress and needs.

There were occasions, however, when everyone's attendance was required at a meeting. An astute project manager, Vani anticipated these meetings and provided her staff advance notice when they all needed to be in the office for three-way video calls.

The schedule worked satisfactorily for her team until the company announced an acquisition. As any manager who has gone through a merger or acquisition can tell you, everything changes the moment the change is announced. For internal communication teams, work expands exponentially and the ability to work as a nimble and seamless team becomes critical. Additionally, more impromptu meetings are often necessary.

Most of Vani's meetings now required real-time input from everyone. The variations in work schedules were no longer practical for the business and loosened the fabric of her team's ability to work and deliver news in a timely manner. Thus, she needed to call for an all-hands-on-deck period, ending flexible scheduling.

...

Priceless Tip #41

The key to making flex scheduling successful is true flexibility, in spirit as well as in fact, from both you and the employee. (Yes, this is the same first sentence of the previous Tip.) If flex scheduling truly interferes with your team's ability to achieve business goals, present the business needs to your team, alerting them as far in advance as you can why they now need to be flexible to the needs of the business.

...

Unfortunately, this flexible schedule blackout phase lasted not just a few months, but for a full year. Several months into that year, one millennial employee quit, stating during the exit interview that having a flexible schedule was one of the primary reasons he had chosen the company over its competitors.

The good news, however, is that the department's employee engagement score averages for the year following the acquisition held steady from the previous year's reported score of 65 percent. Most big data reports show that fewer than 30 percent of the US workforce is truly engaged at work. Vani's explanation of her team's engagement scores remaining well above the international norm:

> *"My team is really into the work and they like working together."*

While both those reasons are probably true, I honestly do not think she gave herself enough credit for the work she invested in building tight relationships with her team. She worked hard to provide them flexible work schedules that matched their life needs. In turn, with the exception of one young employee, they reciprocated when she needed them to give up their personal flexibility.

She also updated them constantly to manage expectations regarding both the increased workload as well when they could see the return of flexible work schedules. As a team, they pulled through this challenging period with Vani rewarding them with virtual parties when they met milestones. She knew her team. Gold stars and internal communication campaign titles such as "Operation Ouch!" were important elements in her management toolbox.

...

Priceless Tip #42

Get to know a manager who is also a millennial.
This person can be a valuable cultural
informant of his/her age cohort's needs.

...

Chapter Six Bonus Exercise

What do you need outside of work to make you feel
rejuvenated and refreshed when you are at work?

Work out a flexible schedule for yourself and treat
yourself to that rejuvenating experience regularly. Tell
your plan to a colleague or your boss – it will help
keep you accountable to your rejuvenation time.

... ...

Chapter Seven

TREAT US LIKE GROWN-UPS!

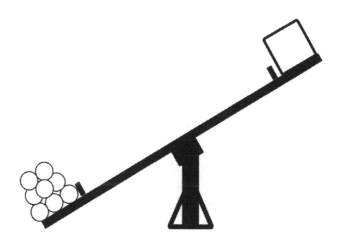

Throughout the findings of our survey and subsequent interviews to learn what millennial employees need in order to be satisfied with their work lives, we regularly encountered stories of frustration with managers who micromanaged. We found an equal number of stories about managers who did not give enough direction.

Amanda encountered these same themes anecdotally while catching up with peers, and even more so when talking to some of her friends from older generations about the challenges they found managing millennial employees.

There is some debate about the causal factors of these two themes. On one hand there is an argument that it is rooted in the same sentiment as the previous chapters: millennial employees are highly motivated by outside measures of success such as titles and defining their current status based on their future status – what they want to be when they are at the peak of their careers.

There is also an argument that they demand the autonomy and expanded responsibility in the workplace because, due to Kindergarten Syndrome beliefs and values, it only seems fair that they would get the same freedom and opportunity that those above them in the organization chart receive.

...

Amanda's "Treat Us Like Grown-Ups!" Experience

My challenges with my first manager were related to pushing back against micromanagement. Before starting my professional life, my type-A personality, competitive nature, and strong-headed demeanor translated into doing well throughout school and in other activities. I received attention from teachers and the ability to work ahead in coursework, which afforded me opportunities to know I had more flexibility than some of my peers. That mattered to my competitive nature.

However, jumping into the real world I did not find myself in an environment with thirty-plus peers in each situation to measure myself against. In that first job there was only one other person at my rank. She had started eighteen months before I did.

Because I didn't have enough objective criteria against which to measure my performance, I felt that my supervisor's micromanaging was a reflection of what she thought of my success (or lack thereof). It actually had nothing to do with me at all. It was, unfortunately, her management style.

...

Priceless Tip #43

If you do not know your management style, strengths, and areas needing improvement, now is the time to learn them. Waiting is not going to make you a more effective manager.

...

Priceless Tip #44

If you have ever heard that you micromanage, you probably do. Get out of denial and learn new people-management skills. Then practice them diligently until they override your default micromanagement style.

...

As Amanda so clearly illustrates above, your youngest employees take your style as a direct measure of the quality of their work. True or not, their perception is their reality and their behavior and responses are based on that subjective reality.

Amanda's Experience, Continued

In my first performance review both my supervisor and her manager, the director, indicated that my number one area for improvement was trusting in my instinct and abilities, and having more confidence in the work that I was doing.

A mere two months after the review I had a huge argument with my supervisor. We had gone through multiple rounds of corrections on a memo. It had gotten to the point where the changes were primarily differences in opinion over minute details such as word choice, or which words of a phrase to bold. By then I felt her goal was more about making me do what she wanted, rather than giving me the tools to be able to grow and complete similar projects on my own in the future.

After nights of working late to get to a level of agreement on that work product, I hit a point where I lost composure. I walked into her office for a final round of reviews and said something to the effect of: "I feel like you wish you hadn't hired me."

Suddenly the conversation was no longer about which word to bold or not. The conversation shifted to the adjustments we needed in our working relationship. In no way did this ultimately fix the challenges we had working together. What it did do, however, was allow me to regain some control over the work that I did accomplish and illustrate to her that the effects of her micromanaging went beyond the project at hand.

...

Priceless Tip #45

Put yourself in the shoes of a super young employee. If this is the employee's first job, your management approach and how you handle each individual challenge will have tremendous impact on this person, well beyond the current challenge.

•••

"I'm micromanaged to the point that "I'm losing confidence in myself..."

•••

"I'm ready to quit now. My manager doesn't believe in my ability to do a great job."

•••

The flip side of micromanaging is a laissez-faire management style. While that style may work for someone who has been in your industry for some time or is mature enough in their career to ask for help or clarification, it simply does not work for young or new employees.

•••

A Case Study About The Dangers of Laissez-Faire Management

Chris G. was a senior level finance professional for a multinational bank. Most of her analysts had been with her for years. They knew the company, their field, and how to work with each other and Chris.

To expand her team, Chris hired a senior analyst who was in her late twenties. The employee looked good on paper, was obviously bright, and was well prepared for the interview. On the surface, she looked like she could hit the ground running, despite her lack of industry experience.

Chris gave her new employee a complex regulatory project and minimal guidance for her first assignment. What Chris did not realize was that this employee was afraid to ask for help. Unfortunately, the narrative section of her report was a disaster. Chris was gentle in her approach to showing the employee the errors in the report. But rather than provide her guidelines for future assignments, Chris suggested she go to other analysts for assistance.

While most employees do not mind helping each other on occasion, Chris' staff felt imposed upon and highly stressed by this obligation. They were a cohesive group but were not open to newbies with endless questions. As a result, this young new employee's constant requests for assistance were not met warmly. Due to their reluctance to help her, she started to ask in an irritable tone and things went from bad to worse. Now the employee had interpersonal problems with her coworkers, which only compounded her performance problem.

Chris' solution? To throw the problem back to her staff to solve with the statement, "I'm sure you all can figure out how to get along."

The new employee perceived that this expectation of autonomy was due to Chris not caring enough about her success to provide the guidance needed to help her grow both in her job and with the seasoned staff. Within six weeks the employee was searching for a new job.

...

Priceless Tip #46

If you have ever heard that you do not provide enough guidance, feedback, or constructive alternatives to your employees, you probably don't.

Similarly, if you have ever heard that you
do not do a stellar job onboarding your
employees, you probably don't.

You need to get out of your comfort zone and
learn to onboard and manage new, especially
younger, employees effectively. They need you.

...

Amanda's Managerial Experience

While you may think we are all sitting at our desks screaming like two-year-olds, "treat us like adults!" that behavior is often more pronounced in the earlier stages of our career.

I had the privilege of working in a management role very early in my career. I was far from perfect at it initially, but my crash course in management proved to be very impactful.

As I discuss the challenges of my generation with older friends I am regularly reminded of one particular learning experience. When I was working as a manager in marketing and business development, the president hired a young woman fresh out of college. I was impressed with her as an entry-level employee but he made the same mistake with her that he had made with me.

When I was ready to move up into my first management role, he had me making critical business decisions before I was ready. I was relatively new in a company and had very little experience in the industry. This young woman was ready to shine in her first entry-level position out of college. Instead her role was to head up a completely new division of the company.

She reported directly to me. I struggled constantly with her naivety and inexperienced approach to the real world. Finally, after having her miss yet another deadline because she had not yet developed the project management skills needed to juggle multiple pressures from multiple people, I lost all patience.

I gathered sticky notes and a marker from my desk and stormed into her office. I wrote down each of the projects we had open and then organized them according deadline and priority on the blank wall behind her desk. In my mind I was treating her like a child, certainly not an approach I would recommend to anyone in a guidance position. I was acting in frustration, straying far from my best self. As I was nearing completion of the task that I viewed as so elementary it would surely insult her, she walked into the office.

What happened next completely surprised me. To this day it has had far-reaching effects on my approach to managing others. She was thrilled! She looked at the sticky notes and for the first time she felt she had the tools to manage her time and priorities. It was the complete opposite of the response I was expecting. She continued using this system long after I left the company. She formalized it using a large dry-erase board and magnets.

My frustration was completely diffused by the surprise I experienced in response to her reaction. The more I thought about it, I realized that she had demanded independence because of the illusion created by being given a "grown-up" position far beyond what she was prepared for. But what she actually needed most at that moment was some basic guidance to help her grow into the position she believed she deserved.

...

Insight From Amanda

Take a step away from being frustrated with your millennial employees who want more autonomy, more guidance, or more of something else and provide each one what s/he needs to be successful.

Our parents told us how special we were but they also held our hand every step of the way. We may be inclined to stomp our feet and scream "treat us like adults!" But don't let that foot stomping distract you from your ultimate goal of cultivating us infant professionals into what we are striving to be – successful adult professionals.

...

A Case Study: "Treat Us Like Grown-Ups!"

Ryan Joiner owns Athlon Fitness & Performance in San Luis Obispo, California. While known as the go-to fitness expert in the region, he is also a voracious adopter of best practices in business. With nine fitness centers within a 1.5-mile radius, Ryan realized early on that he had to offer a value proposition that would keep his business growing. He described his value proposition as:

$$V = CE + R + R^2$$

V: Value: Factors that bring in new customers and encourage current customers to stay

$$=$$

CE: Client Experience: Highly-educated fitness trainers who know their clients' needs and abilities

$$+$$

R: Results: Customers reaching or exceeding their fitness goals

+

R²: Relationships: Between Athlon's highly skilled trainers and their clients, and between Ryan and his staff, which includes four millennial-age employees. Ryan speaks of how relationships are exponentially more important than the other factors. When things are not going as well as they should with a client or that client's results, he examines the relationship his staff has built, or not built, to find solutions.

His approach includes continual development of the technical knowledge and skills his staff needs to be ahead of the curve in providing their clients results. The dreaded-by-all annual performance review does not exist at Athlon. Instead, Ryan provides ongoing, short performance conversations and bi-annual checkups where employees evaluate how well they are living up to the company's core values as a team.

He also holds weekly meetings where he explores the following key performance indicators with his staff:

1. Actions and Results
2. Obstacles and Challenges
3. Questions for the Group

His team knows how well the business is meeting its goals and what they can do to help improve results. They are also invited to contribute ideas. The staff's dedication to relationships, client results, and the business itself is obvious. Although the youngest employees have long-term professional goals beyond Athlon, most of them have been with the company for four to five years and are in no hurry to leave.

...

Malati's View Of Athlon Fitness

There are few fitness centers that impress me as singular in nature. Most are comparable in terms of exercise equipment, fees, and the number of personal trainers to choose from. Athlon is a standout, not just as a fitness and performance center, but also as a business whose value proposition formula is demonstrated by everyone who works there. I have been a client for nearly four years, regularly returning to tune up my exercise program whenever I am in the area. Additionally, I consider my millennial-age Athlon trainer to be an integral part of my health team, on equal footing with the doctors and other health experts that I confer with regularly.

Ryan's formula for fully integrating the youngest members of the workforce into his robust organization is working.

...

Priceless Tip #47

Information is power. Provide your team members
with as much information as you can about
the business, competition, and industry trends.
Invite them to share their insights as well.

...

By now you are probably realizing that although millennial employees are a culturally distinct subgroup, each employee is also a unique individual. Some are smart, wise, and insightful like Amanda. Others may have different gifts.

As a colleague from the UK once told me when my own millennial children were very young:

> *"Each one is like an unusual species of plant. They need different amounts of water, light, and fertilizer."*

Some of your employees may need more direct modeling of an important process. Others may need to learn conflict-management skills. And some may bloom with continual education and business status information.

...

Chapter Seven Bonus Exercise

Take a moment to reminisce about a time when you felt that one of your teachers or early bosses really understood you. What did s/he do that was so different from all the others? How did you feel knowing this person was truly interested in your success?

... ...

Chapter Eight

MORE MONEY PLEASE

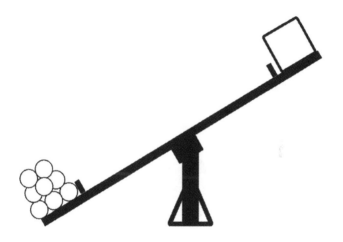

Starting at the bottom of the career ladder almost always means lower compensation. Hence, the desire for higher wages or salaries showed up frequently in the responses to our survey questions.

As we reviewed the comments pertaining to money, we did not see indicators of greed or a sense of entitlement, which is one criticism often made about the millennial cohort. What we saw in the responses was a genuine concern and a degree of fear for economic survival, especially among the youngest respondents. The older respondents who were worried about their financial well-being were concerned they would not be able afford home ownership or savings for retirement like their parents did. Below, from three of our survey questions, is a sample of responses concerning the topic of money:

Question 2: What 2-3 elements have to be in place for you to be willing to stay with your present employer?

...

"Money has to be right"

...

"Competitive pay and benefits"

...

"Livable wages"

...

*"The job must be able not only to pay my bills
but also allow me to save a little money."*

...

*"They just have to pay me and provide the benefits
I need and not piss me off too much."*

...

Question 3: What 2-3 things would make you want to leave your employer?

...

"Poor pay"

...

"Decrease in pay or benefits"

...

"Lack of financial stability"

...

"I'm a planner, so I'd like to be able to plan my finances and schedule ahead of time. This would require my employer not to change my schedule with a phone call the night before."

...

Question 4: What 2-3 things would inspire you to work beyond your typical workday?

...

"More money please"

...

...

"Getting paid overtime"

...

"Opportunity to make more money"

...

Scattered throughout the survey was genuine distress about the challenges of living without sufficient money:

...

"I can't live on this money!"

...

"We have to live four in an apartment, like we're still in college."

...

The need for more money is a key concern to this age cohort, much as it was for their grandparents, many of whom suffered through the Great Depression.

This sense of scarcity is influenced by the economic pressures of the historic recession that hit between 2007 and 2009. Many millennials watched their parents or parents' friends suddenly lose the ability to retire or pay off debt while their homes plummeted in value. Simultaneously, millennials themselves were starting off their adult lives burdened with tremendous college or trade school debt. Some who joined the military came home from service only to find they needed to move in with their parents to make ends meet.

During this time, the goal of earning or maintaining a comfortable living was suddenly out of reach for baby boomers, generation Xers, and millennials alike. Standards for securing home loans were tougher than any time in history and many parents were stretched financially by needing to support their own parents (grandparents to our millennials) over the long term. Also, while in previous generations parents were able to assist their young adult children purchase or make down payments on homes, many millennials found this was no longer the case.

In 2014, the US Bureau of Labor Statistics indicated that the average tenure on the job was only eighteen months for younger millennials and thirty-six months for older millennials. This can be seen in the context of upward mobility being limited in most organizations and wages being insufficient to live on. A fifty-cent-per-hour increase in wage may not seem like much to most salaried managers or business owners. But for a full-time worker of any generation an extra thousand or more dollars each year is a significant consideration when it comes to answering the question, "Where do I want to work?"

If a manager works in an organization owned by other people they may not determine wages and often think they cannot directly influence the amount their employees bring home. This is not always the case.

...

<u>Priceless Tip #48</u>

If you work for a company that is making a profit, you can influence increases in wages or salaries more than you think. Learn how.

...

Malati's Experience Getting Her Staff Salary Increases

I have worked in the various areas of learning and development (L&D) and organization development (OD) for most of my career. As is common in many organizations, if another department performed poorly, the finger was often pointed at L&D. I would be wealthy now if I could monetize the number of times my peers and I have heard one of these complaints from department heads who needed to justify their less than stellar performance: "We didn't have enough training," or, "Our training wasn't good enough."

When there is a dip in profits, L&D and OD are always easy targets for a reduction in force (layoffs). Despite my analytic reports that showed high returns on investment, and direct correlation to increased sales, it was usually challenging for executive management to view L&D/OD as mission critical. Additionally, when the company was doing well, cutting the L&D/OD staff was a great way to squeeze a few more dollars off the next quarter's income statement.

I am a businesswoman first and foremost, and the business I have chosen to be in is learning and organization development. I know the value of a well-run, budget-conscious, high-quality, and creative L&D or OD department to an organization's success. Knowing my department was always at risk of disappearing, I developed two mantras for myself, and utilized them tenaciously, together with my competent staff, whenever I faced internal resistance to organizational improvement:

> *"If an organizational challenge does not have a solution, we will develop one."*

and

> *"Not investing in a known solution to an organizational challenge is quite simply a poor business decision."*

Research has shown that organizations that endorse a learning culture have a competitive advantage to those that do not. Nonetheless, being under intermittent attack and at risk of obsolescence often resulted in my own deepened resolve to succeed, as well as my teams developing "cohesion through adversity."

In my annual budget planning process, I would ensure an increase of my staff's value to the organization by investing in their skill development. We utilized cutting-edge practices in everything we did – project management, root-cause analysis, needs assessments, gap analysis, rapid design and development, delivery solutions, and evaluation practices. Additionally, we documented new best practices that we shared with other L&D/OD professionals at conferences.

We measured everything we did that could correlate back to the company's success. Wherever we could demonstrate direct return on investment, we did. And we were constantly implementing efficiencies, using Lean and Six Sigma practices to increase efficiencies and reduce expenses.

With service level agreements, we achieved buy-in from our business partners to develop learning reinforcement and accountability as part of the learning and employee development cycle. These agreements also helped us manage expectations and reduce finger pointing toward my department if other departments did not meet their goals.

Like any business, we developed a marketing plan that alerted everyone in the company about every great project we worked on, tying everything we did to the organization's business goals.

...

Priceless Tip #49

Do not assume your department's value is going to be obvious to everyone. Build an internal communication plan/marketing plan into every project plan.

...

After I built the business case for the value my department brought to the company, I lobbied to get as large a percentage of the company's compensation increases directed toward my department as possible.

...

Priceless Tip #50

Make it easier for your boss or your executive to work for an increased percentage of the compensation increase pool by providing him/her all the data that proves your department's critical value to the organization's success.

...

Priceless Tip #51

If you are in a department that generates revenue, become superstars! If your department is not at the top of the list but heading that way, make the direct correlation between the employees on your team and your trajectory toward the A-list.

...

Priceless Tip #52

If your department is a cost center, increase productivity, efficiencies, and value to the enterprise. Then make sure everyone who has any influence over compensation decisions knows how your department's value influences the bottom line.

...

Once I became aware of both the approximate percentage and actual dollar amount my department was going to receive from the company compensation pool, I determined how to parse out the increases within my department based on two factors:

1. Who was underpaid for their role (parity)
2. Who was too valuable to lose (merit)

...

Priceless Tip #53

Research what local competition is paying
employees so you can stay competitive.

...

I used the *Cost of Turnover Worksheet* from the Society for Human Resources Management (SHRM) to calculate both the hard costs of replacing an employee and the soft costs, such as increased workload for the rest of the team, their loss of productivity, and my loss of productivity.

According to SHRM research, hard costs of replacing an employee can be up to 60 percent of that employee's annual salary. Total costs can range from 90-200 percent depending on the employee's rank and perceived value to the company.

...

Priceless Tip #54

Determine your turnover costs for your key
employees – before they start thinking about
leaving. Then develop retention and compensation
increase plans for keeping employees.

...

You know from previous chapters how crucial the perception of fairness is to your millennial employees. If your organization is still in the dark ages trying to keep employee wages and salaries secret, become proactive in changing those policies. It is a mistaken notion that employees do not know who is earning more and who is earning less.

Lack of transparency often leads to lack of trust. And, disparities based on sex or other protected classes not only violates federal or state laws, it positions your organization for lawsuits. Your brightest employees will leave and may also file a high-profile class action lawsuit against your company, injuring its reputation.

...

Priceless Tip #55

Do your best to keep your staff informed of your efforts to increase their gross income. Even if you do not achieve the goals you had in mind, just knowing that you are sincerely working on their behalf will build a degree of trust, engagement, and loyalty.

...

The Sharing Economy

Several of our respondents shared with us the trend of employers helping employees earn money on the job site.

One respondent worked as a mechanic for an auto-repair company. The owners of this shop offered the garage to employees during off hours for a minimal rental fee. The employees owned their own tools and were required to secure liability insurance policies. The high-ticket equipment at the shop enabled them to bring in vehicles they were working on for friends or resale.

Another was a graphic designer whose employer allowed use of enterprise-level software licenses for employees to work freelance, outside of business hours. As the respondent's clients were micro-businesses or nonprofits, she was not competing against her employer's company.

In another case, by offering one respondent a flexible schedule, he was able to use the company's commercial kitchen to prep sheets of organic cookies, readying them for baking on the morning of the town's weekly farmers' market.

Moonlighting or having a second job has often been a way employees bring home extra income. Flexible scheduling and permitting employees the use of the company resources benefit both the employees' take-home income and sends a signal to employees that the company values being part of the sharing economy.

If you have been following our Tips from previous chapters, you have already started to build an authentic and healthy manager/millennial team member connection. Always be on the lookout for ways to help your millennial-age, or low-wage employees earn additional income, either within their current role, by preparing them for more senior roles, or by helping them find other sources of income

...

Chapter Eight Bonus Exercise

Earning money and saving money are both aspects of financial health. Ask a financial expert to attend an occasional team meeting to speak on topics concerning saving and investing money: how compounding interest works, how easy it is to "pay yourself first," or how to maximize the company's 401k match or flexible benefits.

...

These are all habits many lower income earners avoid. By teaching your employees that saving does not hurt as they imagined it would, especially if the money is automatically diverted from their paycheck directly into a saving vehicle, you will be doing them a huge favor.

··· ···

Chapter Nine

MY LEMONADE STAND?
THE ENTREPRENEURIAL SPIRIT

Due to the high press coverage of technology's young billionaires, it sometimes feels like millennials are bailing out of their companies and starting their own businesses at record rates. Big data provides conflicting trends, depending on what you read and how you interpret the data. While one report indicates that millennial employees are enthusiastic about starting businesses, another indicates that the number of startups by early career employees is actually lower than it was before millennials entered the workforce.

As Amanda launched her marketing firm before she was twenty-five, we took particular interest in this topic and searched for comments about the urge to start a business amongst our respondents.

When asked what their long-range professional goals were, most of our respondents spoke of achieving greater levels of responsibility or decision-making, and higher compensation. Only a handful specifically mentioned starting a business. Even then, the actual comments sounded less than definitively entrepreneurial.

•••

"Perhaps if the opportunity presented itself, I would like to open my own firm."

•••

"My long-term career goal is to either be a partner at my current firm or start my own practice."

•••

"I'd like to teach at a university. Additionally, I'd like to open a private practice or small collaborative practice."

•••

"... Maybe someday have my own firm. But I really like working with other people, so maybe not."

•••

Only one respondent sounded like a seriously ambitious entrepreneur:

•••

"Long-term career would be to start and manage first two, then twenty, and then fifty companies worth $100 million. Personally, I want to have the option to retire by forty."

•••

Amanda's Experience Becoming a Business Owner

As we have seen, my generation requires of their employers that they be treated equally, given flexibility, and be provided with growth and compensation opportunities. We also have a desire to work in an organization that recognizes and acknowledges our impact. It is important to us too that our jobs create a positive impact on the community, in addition to our personal lives. One great way to achieve all of these demands is to start and grow one's own business.

My own journey began with facing an ethical challenge in the workplace. As much as I can overthink so many other professional decisions, once trust in my boss' ethics was broken, I knew immediately that I needed to leave that job. The question was: what next?

I reached out to my most trusted professional connections to see what opportunities were coming up on the horizon. One of them asked the career-changing question, "Have you thought of starting your own thing?"

At first I scoffed at the idea. I had periodically entertained the notion, but always thought that having my own business was something reserved for later in life. However, the more I thought about it, the more it seemed a good fit. In my own company, I wouldn't have a boss that I would be unhappy with for not having trust in me, or not giving me the tools to be successful, or for micromanaging me, or for violating my trust and ethics.

I was fortunate to have a professional role model who believed in me and helped me believe in myself. Multiple members of my family had started businesses. Some even failed and started again. And, I had the luxury of perfect timing and terrific personal support to build the safety net that allowed me to take the leap into my own business.

It is in my own business that I've finally found a title that I am pleased with and still draw motivation from. It is also in this business that I take pride in the ethics of the company and appreciate the work–life balance.

While running my own business has entailed taking work calls and sneaking in emails during a romantic escape to Hawai'i, I am thrilled with the opportunity to focus my efforts on both the personal and professional aspects of my life. I thrive on the flexibility. I am still occasionally terrified, yet inspired, by the fact that there is no one but myself to blame for my successes and failures.

I've already been a "proprietress" (a title suggested by the baby boomer gentleman who was my father's previous boss) longer than any job I held prior to making the leap. As the company has grown, so has my personal compensation and I've been able to take on employees, and hopefully more in the future.

Considering all of this, I can easily understand why entrepreneurship is so enticing to some members of my generation – it aligns so closely with what we are looking for from our employers.

A number of my peers talk and dream about entrepreneurship. I have one friend who has talked about his frustrations with his job and his plan to start his own company with such conviction that upon hearing him, you'd believe that he's going to do it tomorrow. However, after years of having the same conversation, I see that the pressures and fears of having no one to blame for any aspect of your work life but yourself terrifies him at least as much as it did me, and he has made little headway.

Although most of us will remain employees, I am hopeful that this book will enable managers to assist their millennial employees to live up to their fullest potential.

Working on this book project has instilled in me a sense of pride in my peers. The common theme is not the need to own a business as much as an entrepreneurial *spirit*, a willingness to break the mold and think creatively. When traditional work environments aren't meeting our particular needs, we are willing to push for change or take the risk of leaving a seemingly stable job.

We may not yet know "what we want to be when we grow up," but we know that there is boundless opportunity and that we have the tools to shape that opportunity.

Managers who tap into our dreams and leverage the parameters created by our demanding approach can build environments where we thrive, and will find us more than willing to work hard and smart for the team. Companies that find opportunities to develop key aspects of this entrepreneurial spirit will appeal to their next generation of leaders.

...

Priceless Tip #56

The sooner you realize that your millennial employees do not want to quit, the sooner you will be able to develop yourself into a great manager and mentor for them. If someday later they launch the next hugely disruptive technology, they may invite you to have a role in it. In any case, they will be thankful for your assistance now.

...

The net of our survey responses and Amanda's comments is: your millennial employees are less likely to leave to start their own lemonade stand than they are to leave because their needs are not being met.

...

Chapter Nine Bonus Exercise

If you have ever had an impulse to start a business, join a "hot house" or incubator and explore your idea further. Others with the same inclinations will be there too, including millennials and seasoned experts in the field of assisting startups. Who knows, the energy and available resources may launch you into a new career.

... ...

Chapter Ten

CULTURAL COMPETENCE: MANAGING MILLENNIAL EMPLOYEES

...

"When are they going to get it?"

...

"Why are they so demanding?"

...

You read laments like these earlier in the book and have likely heard other managers complain similarly. Or, you may have said a variation of these statements yourself.

Do millennials really want everything? The short answer: yes and no. As we have read in previous chapters, many have come to expect a similar level of connection to what they were raised with. However, these are not wants; these are cultural needs.

You may recall my epiphany that millennials are a cultural group of eighty million Americans employees (see Chapter One), and our simple definition of culture:

> *"Culture is a set of rules developed by a group of people for survival and success."*

The representatives of this cultural group who responded to our survey and follow-up interviews did not say they want everything. They were, however, quite vocal about what they needed in order to succeed. And, most of them were ready to find work environments that fulfilled their cultural needs. Their cultural needs were developed when they were children, just as ours were.

American culture at its best is built on the framework of freedom of expression, openness, egalitarianism, and challenging stagnate authority. Our millennials hold these same values, but perhaps to a greater degree than previous generational subcultures. In general, unless they are immigrants, or children of immigrants, from ethnic cultures where emotional closeness between adults and children is not the norm, millennial employees successfully navigated their worlds with a great deal of connection with peers, adults, parents, and teachers alike. That basic need will change as they mature, but it will not disappear entirely.

We know from decades of psychological research that some aspects of our personalities can alter as we age. Intercultural studies show that our behaviors adjust as the "rules for survival and success" change from environment to environment. The brain can make new pathways and continue learning throughout our lifespan. Yet each of us has "cultural firmware" that we learned from our families, other important adults in our childhood, media, and institutions. Despite being somewhat malleable, our fundamental personalities and cultural selves are established in early childhood, getting minor "patches," "bridges," and "upgrades" as we age and experience more of life.

What does this mean relative to our ability to become exceptional managers of millennial generation employees? Since we posited the premise that millennials are culturally different than older employees, our conscious shift as managers is to realize that this is just another adjustment to workplace culture. Because baby boomers are such a large population, they have influenced everything around them at each stage of their lives, including the workplace and expectations from their managers. Just as an entirely new paradigm for managing and leading employees developed as the boomer generation flooded into the workplace, now millennials are flooding into offices, warehouses, and workplaces of all types, changing paradigms.

The adjustments required of managers are perfectly normal aspects of the evolution of the global economy. Just as we would adjust our management behaviors accordingly for international colleagues from India, Brazil, or Ireland, or domestic colleagues from Louisiana, Staten Island, or San Francisco, we need to do so for our millennial colleagues as well. And, like our colleagues from other regions of the US or other nations, the longer millennial employees work with us, the more they will adjust too. We are *all* adjusting. By developing cultural competence and understanding the deeper underpinnings of our cultures, we will create new methods for working harmoniously and productively together.

...

Priceless Tips For Managers

By reading the previous chapters, you have taken a short tour of some aspects of the millennial subculture and have listened to millennials themselves. Chapter Eleven wraps this book up with a recap of all the Priceless Tips and Bonus Exercises from each chapter. Collectively, these Tips will help make your journey with millennial employees a more satisfying adventure and help you develop into a more effective manager.

As stated by Dale Carnegie, in his formative 1937 book, *How To Win Friends And Influence People*:

> *"Success in dealing with people depends on a sympathetic grasp of the other person's point of view."*

As you become an increasingly inquisitive and caring manager of each of your employees, you will develop a greater enjoyment of the process and achieve more for yourself, your team members, and your organization. Bon voyage!

...

Chapter Ten Bonus Exercise

Have more fun on your journey of being a manager of millennial employees. You have everything to gain!

... ...

Chapter Eleven

RECAP: 56 PRICELESS TIPS FOR MANAGERS AND TEN BONUS EXERCISES

The following is a recap of the Priceless Tips and Bonus Exercises from each chapter.

••• •••

Chapter One
Confessions Of A Baby Boomer Manager: A Book Is Born

Priceless Tip #1

Use the cultural iceberg framework to understand your millennial employee on a deeper level. It is more effective than inwardly screaming.

Priceless Tip #2

Do not hesitate to ask peers for their ideas. Just don't be surprised if they know less than you do.

Priceless Tip #3

Sincere dialogue means we listen deeply more than we speak.

Priceless Tip #4

Remember this useful definition of culture: "A set of rules developed by a group of people for survival and success." From this definition you will not only gain greater understanding of yourself and your millennial employees, you can also lead the development of your team's optimal working culture.

Chapter One Bonus Exercise

Frame the frustrations you may be feeling managing your millennial employees as growing pains. Often, if we do not recognize that something is not working, we will not search for solutions to improve it. That you are reading this book indicates you are on the continuous process-improvement journey – the process of becoming a more effective manager. Congratulate yourself!

··· ···

Chapter Two
We Can't Write The Book Yet: The Research Phase

Priceless Tip #5

Knowledge is not as important as understanding.

Priceless Tip #6

Millennial employees belong to a truly different subculture than their older managers. Be prepared to shift gears to accommodate and bridge these cultural differences.

Priceless Tip #7

In order to build a workplace culture in which everyone can thrive, respect the "rules for survival and success" of your employees.

Chapter Two Bonus Exercise

Managers on multiple continents are facing the same challenges you are. As they develop and share practices that work with us, we will pass them along in social media posts or blog articles. Please send us what works for you as well. We would be thrilled to share your success stories too.

··· ···

Chapter Three
The Kindergarten Syndrome

Priceless Tip #8

Do not assume you understand the meaning of what your employee is saying just because you are both using the same words in the same language.

Priceless Tip #9

Millennials, especially the younger ones, need more "Gold Stars" than older employees. Give them out generously, even if it is just for their hard work.

Priceless Tip #10

Anticipate in advance that good news for one employee may not feel like good news for another employee.

Priceless Tip #11

Before giving an employee public recognition, make sure you know it will be welcomed by the employee and not be a source of embarrassment.

Chapter Three Bonus Exercise

Create an informal spreadsheet with the name of each employee in column A. In column B, indicate what you think each employee's personalized Gold Star might be.

··· ···

Chapter Four
What Do We Want To Be When We Grow Up?
Career Development

Priceless Tip #12

Accept it. You have an important role to play in your millennial employees' lives.

Priceless Tip #13

Take each of your staff members out for lunch once in a while. It does not have to be fancy or expensive. It just needs to be dedicated one-on-one time.

Priceless Tip #14

As each work group is unique, develop ways to create an atmosphere of connection for your particular group.

Priceless Tip #15

Show each employee that you care about his/her future, however s/he defines it.

Priceless Tip #16

Be an active career counselor to your millennial employees. And, share your own career journey. Perhaps they can avoid some of the mistakes you've made.

Priceless Tip #17

Upgrade your consulting skills so you can be a supportive manager. Learn about your millennial employees' short- and long-term goals.

Priceless Tip #18

Start career conversations by asking questions such as, "If you could do anything in the world, what would it be?"

Priceless Tip #19

Help your employees achieve their dreams. Work with them to set up a clear development path that will get them to where they want to go. And, introduce them to your professional network to help expand theirs.

Priceless Tip #20

Tie it together for them. Discuss how your employees' current roles and next steps fit into their career goals, your department's goals, and the organization's big-picture goals.

Priceless Tip #21

Insert "Career Goals" on the agenda of a work-group meeting occasionally. By encouraging open dialogue about mid- and long-term goals, members of your work group can become resources for each other. It's also a great move toward building a cohesive team.

Chapter Four Bonus Exercise

Ask your employees to give themselves titles that reflect their future selves: a role they may hold sometime in their career or family life in the future. Then invite them to print and post their new titles in/on their workspace or uniform.

··· ···

Chapter Five
Yeah Team! The Work Environment

<u>Priceless Tip #22</u>

Expect many of your younger employees to want to work together more often than to work as individual contributors.

<u>Priceless Tip #23</u>

Create small project teams whenever you see the opportunity.

<u>Priceless Tip #24</u>

Learn to be more tolerant of what your generation may have considered "immature" behavior in the workplace.

<u>Priceless Tip #25</u>

As much as you may hate confrontation, managing the behavior of your staff and holding employees accountable for how they act is critical for developing an enjoyable, tension-free, and productive environment.

<u>Priceless Tip #26</u>

Pay attention to undercurrents of dissatisfaction or active disengagement amongst members of project teams. If you sense something is off, or if someone complains about another team member, immediately address the situation. The following tip has nine steps you can use to assist an employee to improve his/her behavior.

<u>Priceless Tip #27</u>

Employ these nine steps to coach employees who need to improve their behavior:

1. Describe the employee's negative behavior.
2. Describe the impact the behavior has on the group's ability to achieve its goals.
3. Ask the employee to provide 1-2 viable solutions toward correcting the behavior, then add your own ideas.
4. Explain to the employee what may happen next if s/he does not correct the behavior.
5. Make sure you have a verbal indication that your employee understands the importance of the changes needed and is willing to make those changes.
6. Set a schedule to touch base and review progress once each week, or more frequently if necessary.
7. Follow up with an email detailing all elements of the conversation.
8. Keep your commitment to meet with the employee as scheduled.
9. Give the employee kudos for small wins as s/he develops the more positive behaviors.

Priceless Tip #28

If you have ever been given feedback that you micromanage or are a boss who is difficult to get along with, improve your interpersonal and people-management skills immediately through learning and practice. And, get a coach to assist you gain mastery of your new skills faster.

Priceless Tip #29

If you have not had the opportunity to experience a 360-degree multi-rater feedback process, find a valid and reliable feedback tool and have your boss, colleagues, and direct reports provide you feedback. If you have obtained 360-degree feedback, conduct the survey again with your current team.

Priceless Tip #30

Establish an accountability partnership with another manager and use peer-to-peer coaching to improve whatever behaviors you may be exhibiting that would give your low-tolerance millennial employees reason to leave.

Chapter Five Bonus Exercise

Interview an intercollegiate athletic coach to learn ways to create a cohesive team atmosphere.

··· ···

Chapter Six
Growing Up In A Digital World:
Communication And Flexibility

Priceless Tip #31

"We millennials don't want to be placed into situations based on what you think you know about us." - Amanda

Priceless Tip #32

In addition to the obvious caution of not stereotyping all millennial employees as having any single characteristic, remember that each one is a unique person first.

Priceless Tip #33

Establish a strong, honest relationship with your boss. There are a multitude of reasons for this critical relationship, not the least of which is the ability to confer on a sensitive topic before one of your employees does.

Priceless Tip #34

Make sure your values are in alignment with your organization's values and expectations. If your company supports flexible work schedules and it is part of the organizational culture, learn how and when it can be beneficial to your team's employee engagement and productivity.

Priceless Tip #35

If you sincerely cannot work within your company's values, expectations, and organizational culture, consider changing companies. It will save you a lot of stress and prevent a potential epidemic of staff exits.

Priceless Tip #36

Meet with each of your employees to determine each one's flexibility needs. Then be sincere in your attempt to meet these needs. Reasonable employees will appreciate you taking the first step toward meeting their needs and will negotiate something that will not compromise work goals.

Priceless Tip #37

If your organization does not yet embrace flexible scheduling, take a leadership role in establishing it by conducting a proof-of-concept experiment with a member or two of your team.

Priceless Tip #38

Communicating with your employees who are working elsewhere remains important. When they are "on the clock" treat them as you would any on-site employee.

Priceless Tip #39

Learn to text. For your millennial employees especially, texting is an efficient way to communicate that guarantees quick answers to your questions.

Priceless Tip #40

The key to making flex scheduling successful is true flexibility, in spirit as well as in fact, from both you and the employee. Millennial employees will be going through many life-stage transitions. Working with them to determine flexible work arrangements can strengthen your relationships and their engagement with their jobs.

Priceless Tip #41

The key to making flex scheduling successful is true flexibility, in spirit as well as in fact, from both you and the employee. (Yes, this is the same first sentence of the previous Tip.) If flex scheduling truly interferes with your team's ability to achieve business goals, present the business needs to your team, alerting them as far in advance as you can why they now need to be flexible to the needs of the business.

Priceless Tip #42

Get to know a manager who is also a millennial. This person can be a valuable cultural informant of his/her age cohort's needs.

Chapter Six Bonus Exercise

What do you need outside of work to make you feel rejuvenated and refreshed when you are at work?

Work out a flexible schedule for yourself and treat yourself to that rejuvenating experience regularly. Tell your plan to a colleague or your boss – it will help keep you accountable to your rejuvenation time.

··· ···

Chapter Seven
Treat Us Like Grown-Ups!

Priceless Tip #43

If you do not know your management style, strengths, and areas needing improvement, now is the time to learn them. Waiting is not going to make you a more effective manager.

Priceless Tip #44

If you have ever heard that you micromanage, you probably do. Get out of denial and learn new people-management skills. Then practice them diligently until they override your default micromanagement style.

Priceless Tip #45

Put yourself in the shoes of a super young employee. If this is the employee's first job, your management approach and how you handle each individual challenge will have tremendous impact on this person, well beyond the current challenge.

Priceless Tip #46

If you have ever heard that you do not provide enough guidance, feedback, or constructive alternatives to your employees, you probably don't.

Similarly, if you have ever heard that you do not do a stellar job onboarding your employees, you probably don't.

You need to get out of your comfort zone and learn to onboard and manage new, especially younger, employees effectively. They need you.

Priceless Tip #47

Information is power. Provide your team members with as much information as you can about the business, competition, and industry trends. Invite them to share their insights as well.

Chapter Seven Bonus Exercise

Take a moment to reminisce about a time when you felt that one of your teachers or early bosses really understood you. What did s/he do that was so different from all the others? How did you feel knowing this person was truly interested in your success?

••• •••

Chapter Eight
More Money Please

Priceless Tip #48

If you work for a company that is making a profit, you can influence increases in wages or salaries more than you think. Learn how.

Priceless Tip #49

Do not assume your department's value is going to be obvious to everyone. Build an internal communication plan/marketing plan into every project plan.

Priceless Tip #50

Make it easier for your boss or your executive to work for an increased percentage of the compensation increase pool by providing him/her all the data that proves your department's critical value to the organization's success.

Priceless Tip #51

If you are in a department that generates revenue, become superstars! If your department is not at the top of the list but heading that way, make the direct correlation between the employees on your team and your trajectory toward the A-list.

Priceless Tip #52

If your department is a cost center, increase productivity, efficiencies, and value to the enterprise. Then make sure everyone who has any influence over compensation decisions knows how your department's value influences the bottom line.

Priceless Tip #53

Research what local competition is paying employees so you can stay competitive.

Priceless Tip #54

Determine your turnover costs for your key employees – before they start thinking about leaving. Then develop retention and compensation increase plans for keeping employees.

Priceless Tip #55

Do your best to keep your staff informed of your efforts to increase their gross income. Even if you do not achieve the goals you had in mind, just knowing that you are sincerely working on their behalf will build a degree of trust, engagement, and loyalty.

Chapter Eight Bonus Exercise

Earning money and saving money are both aspects of financial health. Ask a financial expert to attend an occasional team meeting to speak on topics concerning saving and investing money: how compounding interest works, how easy it is to "pay yourself first," or how to maximize the company's 401k match or flexible benefits.

··· ···

Chapter Nine
My Lemonade Stand? The Entrepreneurial Spirit

Priceless Tip #56

The sooner you realize that your millennial employees do not want to quit, the sooner you will be able to develop yourself into a great manager and mentor for them. If someday later they launch the next hugely disruptive technology, they may invite you to have a role in it. In any case, they will be thankful for your assistance now.

Chapter Nine Bonus Exercise

If you have ever had an impulse to start a business, join a "hot house" or incubator and explore your idea further. Others with the same inclinations will be there too, including millennials and seasoned experts in the field of assisting startups. Who knows, the energy and available resources may launch you into a new career.

··· ···

Chapter Ten
Cultural Competence:
Managing Millennial Employees

Chapter Ten Bonus Exercise

Have more fun on your journey of being a manager of millennial employees. You have everything to gain!

··· ···

Chapter Twelve

RESOURCES

Articles about millennial employees and their managers are forwarded to us constantly. As interest in these topics remains strong, we continue to read nearly every article, blog post, or editorial that comes our way.

You can keep up with workplace trends through any of the primary resources listed alphabetically below.

- Council of Economic Advisors for the President of the United States
- Deloitte LLP
- Gallup, Inc.
- Pew Research Center
- Society for Human Resources Management (SHRM)

- SHRM Foundation
- US Chamber of Commerce
- US Census Bureau
- US Department of Labor
- US Equal Employment Opportunity Commission
- World Future Society

••• •••

Chapter Thirteen

ABOUT THE AUTHORS

Malati Marlene Shinazy, MEd

Malati (rhymes with "quality") is the baby boomer mother of children born in both the Gen X and millennial generations. A fifth-generation native of San Francisco, California, Malati's ancestors came to the US from the Philippines, China, Spain, Africa, Scotland, Ireland, France, and Eastern Europe. From this unusual family mix, Malati developed an early interest in how people from different cultures learn to function with a degree of harmony.

She earned her BA in Psychology, minoring in Cultural Anthropology and Theatre at University of California, Davis.

Her Master of Education degree was conferred by Cabrini College in Radnor, Pennsylvania.

For nearly twenty years Malati has worked worldwide as an external consultant as well as within organizations as Chief Learning Officer and Organization Development Officer, with expertise in the fields of diversity and inclusion, and leadership development. She is the principal of Pacific Leadership Consultants.

Malati's publications include:

- Author of "Cultural Self-Awareness In Leadership Teams," in the book *Global Competence: 50 Activities for Succeeding in International Business* (HRD Press)
- Expert in *Working Together II, Succeeding in a Multicultural Workplace* (Crisp Publications DVD)
- Developer of TeenDIVERSOPHY™, an intercultural learning game for high school and young college students

Malati is the subject matter expert on the millennial generation of employees for the Association for Talent Development's Management Community of Practice. She is also on the board of directors of the Santa Barbara Human Resources Association chapter of SHRM and was honored as 2015 Member of the Year for her work advancing the human resources profession.

When not traveling for business, Malati is welcomed home to Hilo, Hawai'i by Jean Guillaume and the hordes of Puerto Rican coquí frogs that surround their home. Off-work activities include advocating for public awareness and research of autoimmune myositis diseases and paddling her custom double-outrigger canoe.

Amanda S. Diefenderfer

Amanda was born in 1987, smack in the middle of the millennial generation. While studying for her BS in Commerce with a focus in marketing, she also received a BA in English from Santa Clara University, California.

Having grown up in the wine industry, and in preparing to return to the industry, she noticed that studies of generational motivations within the industry showed an unexpected surge in millennials' adoption of wine purchasing and consumption at a younger age and at a higher rate than preceding generations.

From these early roots, Amanda continued to seek out opportunities to talk with peers and business leaders about the behaviors, strengths, and challenges of working with millennials. In her first management position she experienced these first hand as she managed a team that spread across several generations.

In 2012 she began her company, Big Red Marketing. One of her first clients was coauthor Malati Marlene Shinazy, who was launching Pacific Leadership Consultants. In conversations that continued beyond the initial project they discovered similar passions for sharing experiences and recommendations to those collaborating with the millennial generation in the workplace. With this discovery, some of the core concepts of the book came to life.

Today, Amanda is thrilled to have grown Big Red Marketing with new team members and clients across the wine, tourism, and lifestyle industries.

Amanda lives in Arroyo Grande, California with her husband, Joe, and their corgi, Napoleon. Her passion outside of work is training with her show-jumping horse, RV There Yet?

··· ···

Authors' Contact Information

Malati Marlene Shinazy, MEd
Pacific Leadership Consultants
+1.415.828.0321
mshinazy@p-l-cs.com
www.pacificleadershipconsultants.com
@malati_shinazy

Amanda S. Diefenderfer
Big Red Marketing
+1.805.610.6325
adief@bigredmktg.com
www.bigredmktg.com
@BigRedMktg

Printed in the United States
By Bookmasters